Walking the Line

Walking the Line

Embracing the Imperatives of Jesus

Alan Davey

WIPF & STOCK · Eugene, Oregon

WALKING THE LINE
Embracing the Imperatives of Jesus

Copyright © 2021 Alan Davey. All rights reserved. Except for brief quotations in critical publications or reviews, no part of this book may be reproduced in any manner without prior written permission from the publisher. Write: Permissions, Wipf and Stock Publishers, 199 W. 8th Ave., Suite 3, Eugene, OR 97401.

Wipf & Stock
An Imprint of Wipf and Stock Publishers
199 W. 8th Ave., Suite 3
Eugene, OR 97401

www.wipfandstock.com

PAPERBACK ISBN: 978-1-7252-9034-1
HARDCOVER ISBN: 978-1-7252-9035-8
EBOOK ISBN: 978-1-7252-9036-5

OCTOBER 19, 2021

The Scripture quotations in this publication are from the New Revised Standard Version, ©1989, Division of Christian Education of the National Council of the Churches of Christ in the U.S.A. Used by permission.

Illustrations used in this book with the permission of Joy Kim's estate.

Contents

About the Artist and the Art | vii

INTRODUCTION: *Walking the Line* | ix

PART I: CASTING THE VISION

Chapter 1	Launching Out into the Deep	3
Chapter 2	The Lightness of Being: Laying Down One's Burdens	15
Chapter 3	The Black Hole of Anxiety	26
Chapter 4	The Enigma of the Downward Way	39

PART II: GOING DEEPER

Chapter 5	The Way of the True Self	53
Chapter 6	An Anchored Faith	65
Chapter 7	The Dangers of Judgmentalism	77
Chapter 8	Love Is Something That You Do	89

PART III: MOVING TO MATURITY

Chapter 9	Authentic Discipleship	103
Chapter 10	Salt and Light: Two Metaphors for the People of God	115
Chapter 11	Turning the World Upside Down: Moving from Pride to Humility	128
Chapter 12	Power of Duplication	139

EPILOGUE | 152

Bibliography | 157

About the Artist and the Art

Joy Elizabeth Kim
Have You Walked in My Shoes?

WHEN I WAS IN THE MIDDLE of this project I was asked to conduct the funeral for my wife's niece, Joy Kim, who died prematurely. She was an extraordinary person—an elementary teacher, musician, and visual artist with deep sensitivity. She loved God with a passion and resonated with his even deeper love for each person. Out of her own personal suffering she had transformed her observations into whimsical and imaginative pictures, striking and, at times, puzzling, in their vibrant colors. While sitting with her family after the memorial service, I leafed through a collection of her recent exhibition "Have You Walked in My Shoes." I immediately made a connection with my thoughts on "walking the line" with her haunting pictures of footwear. These shoes and boots and slippers can represent disciples who embrace Jesus's imperatives in the everyday of their lives.

From the Artist's Statement

"When I drew these pictures, I thought about all the different types of people from Las Vegas that Verve Church was reaching out to. There are pictures representing homelessness. There is a ballerina, a cowboy, a couple from the military, another couple who adopt children. There are kids' shoes, boots, running shoes. Each picture has its own story . . ."

About the Artist and the Art

Chapter 1	"Run for Your Life!"
Chapter 2	"In Honor of Military Wives: 'I am waiting for you'"
Chapter 3	"Foster Dad: Ruben"
Chapter 4	"In Honor of Veterans in Wheel Chairs"
Chapter 5	"Foster Mom: Michelle"
Chapter 6	"Cowboy Boots"
Chapter 7	"Please Don't Put me in the Spotlight"
Chapter 8	"Man's Work Shoes"
Chapter 9	"Dear Christian Lady in High Heels"
Chapter 10	"To the Unknown Soldier: My Hero"
Chapter 11	"Just Kids"
Chapter 12	"Ballerina Slippers"
On the cover	"To the Unknown Soldier: My Hero"

Joy comments on "Please Don't Put Me in the Spotlight," *By the way, this is me.* Don't ask me to talk in front of large crowds. I used to stutter when I was a kid. Then I learned how to sing, and I stopped stuttering."

Introduction

Walking the Line

I FIRST CAME ACROSS THE PHRASE "walking the line" when I was a music student in the jazz program at Humber College in Toronto in the 1970s. I remember playing in an ensemble where the group became a bit rambunctious toward the end of the song. The professor called out, "Bring it down, guys. Just 'walk the line.'" What he meant by that quip was to simplify the playing and bring the song home to a restful conclusion. The idea has stayed with me over the years. There is a place to keep something simple and just "walk the line." Sometimes less is more. The spaces between the notes are as important as the notes themselves.

When I reflect upon this truth I think the same can be said for preaching. We don't need to impress everyone with a barrage of theological jargon and complicated language. More often than not, simply "walking the line" in the presentation of the gospel is far more effective than elaborate ideas and eloquent language. We do just that when we tell the stories of Jesus, and these stories naturally lead to serious reflection upon his imperatives noted in the Gospels.

What is the Master Teacher really about as he leads his disciples into a deeper understanding and practice concerning the kingdom of God? His disciples are not scholars, but regular folk from a cross section of trades, and Jesus desires to lead them into a growing relationship with himself, and indeed, his Father Abba. He doesn't want to lose them by elucidating upon sophisticated philosophical concepts—even if they are true! Rather, he keeps it simple by laying out kingdom precepts and doing so by highlighting the core dynamics of the God-human relationship.

Introduction

The Gospels are vital sources of revelation from the mouth of Christ; all four Gospels are rich offerings of wisdom and insight. But for the purposes of this book, we are going to focus on the Gospel of Matthew. In Matthew's account Jesus is presented as the coming king of God's Messianic kingdom who gives directives to active and potential disciples. Jesus's exhortations or commands will shape our reflections. We know from our own schooling that when a teacher makes a specific direction our ears perk up because we know a crucial point is coming our way. The same is true with the teachings of Jesus. His commands are meant to wake us up. They highlight the critical steps to light up our path. Furthermore, it is essential to understand that the instruction of the Master Teacher is not limited to head knowledge. Jesus's commands speak to all of life, including head and heart, understanding and practice, speech and action. This is particularly demonstrated in the powerful discourse from Matthew known as "The Sermon on the Mount" (Matt 5–7) where we hear the Master's clarion call on a series of significant life issues.

Jesus's tutelage is not obscure or archaic. It continues to speak in a powerful and insightful manner to the contemporary issues of our day and does so by outlining a way of clarity, simplicity, love, and peace. Where the secular world presents division, Jesus speaks of unity. Where the world acclaims dominating power, Jesus announces humble service. Where the world emphasizes self-centered egoism, Jesus highlights the path of sacrificial love. The road that Jesus walks and instructs his followers to pursue is a road shaped by awareness, self-knowledge, and personal growth. It is, indeed, a way of fecundity. It is characterized by abundance as we walk in relationship with a loving God who travels with us in intimate conversation. Finally, it is a generative and fruitful path as we mature in our understanding as children of our gracious God.

Having said that, we still might ask whether it is really necessary to study the commands of Christ. What value is there in such an exercise? Shouldn't we just get on with the task of helping others in practical ways that really make a difference? My response to such questions is a wholehearted yes! It is unquestionably helpful to consider the dynamic words of Jesus! We forget him so quickly. The commonplace platitude "out of sight out of mind" applies not just to people we see and know, but also to our Father in heaven. We are conditioned constantly by the values of our noisy world and we find substitutes for our Leader in a plethora of interests and desires. Subsequently we become tired Christians who suffer from a lack

Introduction

of conviction, authenticity, and prophetic insight. Ergo, I reassert the value and importance of hearing and then obeying the commands of Jesus for both our individual selves and for our community of faith.

When we are newly awakened to Jesus's imperatives we can "walk the line" comfortably and in a rhythm that fosters advancement, enjoyment, and heartfelt acceptance. Of course, we must declare our "yes" in an ongoing manner to the overtures of Abba's love. It is an invitation (not a hardship!) to be directed by Jesus. As the Epistle of James reminds us, "Draw near to God, and he will draw near to you" (4:8). As we awaken to the God of love there is a magnetic attraction that draws us into his loving arms. The prophet Jeremiah alludes to this attractive quality when he encourages us to follow the course: "Where the good way lies . . . walk in it, and find rest for your souls" (6:16). And so it is in this good way, taught by the Wonderful Counselor, that we open up our hearts and minds and "walk the line" with Jesus.

Part I

Casting the Vision

Chapter 1

Launching Out into the Deep

The heart of sin is that we do not let ourselves be loved by God; in other words, that we do not let God be God. Normally, this refusal to let God be God, be love, does not happen explicitly, but through our lifestyle, which in turn is determined by the order of our priorities.

Peter Van Breemen

Let All God's Glory Through, 24-25

Now when Jesus heard that John had been arrested, he withdrew to Galilee. He left Nazareth and made his home in Capernaum by the lake, in the territory of Zebulun and Naphtali, so that what had been spoken through the prophet Isaiah might be fulfilled:

> *"Land of Zebulun, land of Naphtali, on the road by the sea, across the Jordan, Galilee of the Gentiles—the people who sat in darkness have seen a great light, and for those who sat in the region and shadow of death light has dawned."*

From that time Jesus began to proclaim, "Repent, for the kingdom of heaven has come near."

As he walked by the Sea of Galilee, he saw two brothers, Simon, who is called Peter, and Andrew his brother, casting a net into the lake—for they were fisherman. And he said to them, "Follow me, and I will make you fish for people." Immediately they left their nets and followed him. As he went from there, he saw two other brothers, James son of Zebedee and his brother John, in the boat with their

Part I: Casting the Vision

father Zebedee, mending their nets, and he called them. Immediately they left the boat and their father, and followed him.

Jesus went throughout Galilee, teaching in their synagogues and proclaiming the good news of the kingdom and curing every disease and every sickness among the people. So his fame spread throughout all Syria, and they brought to him all the sick, those who were afflicted with various diseases and pains, demoniacs, epileptics, and paralytics, and he cured them. And great crowds followed him from Galilee, the Decapolis, Jerusalem, Judea, and from beyond the Jordan. (Matt 4:12–25)

Diving the isolated waters of Little Cayman one can safely enjoy the shallow reef with its myriad of fish life and beautiful turquoise waters. It is relaxing, stress-free, peaceful, and dynamic in its own way. But the magic of Little Cayman is not found in the shallows. It is revealed in the deep blue waters falling off Bloody Bay Wall that descend three miles into the subterranean world. Here one finds ancient sponges, canyons, crevices, and a rock face painted over with diverse corals of every shape and color imaginable. It is there for the taking, but to enjoy it, one has to dive over the top of the wall and descend into the dark blue depths. It feels risky, perhaps a bit crazy, but that is where the magic lies.

Following the way of Christ has a similar feel at first. We may muse, "Do I really want to exchange my comfortable life in the shallows for a scary descent into the unknown? Why would I do that? My life is mostly a peaceful ride, even if somewhat prosaic. At least I can touch bottom when necessary. Let's leave the deep waters for the zealots and safely frolic in the security of the shallow waters."

Jesus understands our hesitancy. Nevertheless, he calls us to push out into the deep. He invites us to take the risk and go over the top of the wall and down into the depths of knowing and experiencing the Divine Mystery. We face this conundrum every day. Do we restrain ourselves, dictated by our culture that promotes a focus on our own desires? Or do we become risk-takers and follow the divine overture into the deeper waters of inner abundance and true serenity? Indeed, Jesus bids us to join his group of disciples and enter his school of training. His desire is that the voice of the Father—one he knows so well—might become the muse that leads us in the way of reclaiming our birthright as children of our loving, eternal God.

The Gift of Reorientation

Jesus begins his public ministry by echoing the words of his cousin John, "Repent, for the kingdom of heaven has come near" (Matt 4:17). These are not meant to be the frightening words that we might imagine today. A call to repentance is not proffered to raise up depictions of fire and brimstone but is an invitation to enter into abundant life. Repentance, which in the Greek is *metanoia*, draws its meaning from the Hebrew *shub*, and simply means "to turn"—to turn away from a set of self-centered priorities to a new viewpoint where God holds the foundational position. Before coming into a relationship with God, our self-centered interests are our core desires. What we want and what benefits us are the only things that matter. When we turn to God (repent) we recognize that there is a better way—one that may be costly—but ultimately, a way of love that flows between God and us and then out to our neighbor.

Of course, turning to God isn't a one-time event. There is an imperative to keep turning to him over and over. It is true that we often have a particular conversion moment when we say our "yes" to God and make a pivotal choice to open our lives up to him. But the choice needs to be reaffirmed each day. Being in a relationship with God is meant to be our everyday experience. For this to take place we need, in the words of Richard Rohr, to "*unlearn* a lot."[1] There is a need to create new habits that help us in our desire to know and say "yes" to God. It means that we have to spend time with other followers of God—other people who desire to live within the new rubric of love. Perhaps, it is necessary to make new friendships and enter new support circles.

We need to be diligent if we are going to truly open ourselves up to Divine Love. There is no room for holding onto the old ways of selfish gratification, stepping on others to get ahead, playing the world's game of personal ambition, and holding on to a hierarchical model. If we keep doing these things then what is the nature of our "turning?" No, repentance is serious business. Jesus announces, "Repent, for the kingdom of heaven has come near." His declaration calls for a recognition of the King's kingdom that surpasses in every way our former selfish concerns. We embark on a journey, a process of unlearning our old destructive ways, and learning the fruitful new ways of loving our loving Father, ourselves, and our brothers and sisters who share our earthly home.

---

1. Rohr, *Falling Upward*, x.

Part I: Casting the Vision

Loving God is crystallized in loving Jesus. We affirm that God reveals himself best in the person of his Son. As Matthew records, at Jesus's baptism the Spirit of God descended from heaven as a dove and alighted upon him, and a voice from heaven declared that Jesus is his Beloved Son in whom he is well pleased (Matt 3:16–17). Since the mystery of God is incarnated in human form in the person of Jesus, as we come to know him we come to know the Father. As a result, the path forward in the journey of repentance is worked out in our friendship with Jesus. He is the one who reveals the nature of the Father. He is the one who opens his heart to us so that we are able to grow into maturity as the Father's beloved children. As Matthew declares, Jesus is the light of God (4:16), who as Isaiah presaged, becomes for us "Wonderful Counselor, Mighty God, Everlasting Father, Prince of Peace" (Isa 9:6). Looking to Jesus becomes the way of continuing our work of reorientation so that the old self fades away and the new creation in Jesus blossoms.

Entering the School of Christ

As Jesus calls people to repentance he begins to form his band of disciples. Walking along the shores of the Sea of Galilee he spots two brothers, Simon and Andrew, casting their net into the waters. He calls out to them, "Follow me, and I will make you fish for people" (Matt 4:19), and surprisingly, the brothers immediately leave their nets and follow. Farther along the shore, Jesus repeats his invitation, appealing to two more fishermen, James and John, who also leave their nets and follow him (4:21). It is striking that Jesus begins his selection process from his immediate environs. He does not scrutinize dozens of applications from prospective disciples; rather, he begins exactly where he finds himself—summoning fishermen who are plying their trade along the shores of his home town. (Curiously, this approach might just be the best for future discipleship programs. Who are the interested and available persons for ministry in our own context? Before looking for a superstar from afar it might be more beneficial to identify persons in our own circle who share our passion for God's kingdom.)

As we step back and reflect on this early narrative, we note that Jesus's ministry holds two salient imperatives: First, he invites the broader community to repent (turn) from their self-centered ways and open their hearts to the Father's love (Matt 4:17). Second, he calls individuals to follow him—"Come after me" (4:19)—and enter the new school he is establishing.

Together the commands are an invitation to "wake up"—to open their hearts and minds to the deeper truths of life. This invitation is extended to us all. May we see beyond the exigencies of life to seize the vocation that vivifies and enlightens our existence.

It is true that it is not an easy road, but a radical call demanding full commitment. In the familiar words of Dietrich Bonhoeffer, it is a challenge "to come and die."[2] We are to die to the world's lust for power, its desperation for prestige and honor, and its glorification of ego. Alas, we are not always prepared to let the old ways go. Further in Matthew's Gospel, we observe Jesus extending his invitation to a young zealous individual who is full of creative potential. Yet, he declines the call to join Jesus's band due to his riches. He chooses comfort and convenience over a life of adventure with the upside-down strategies of the King of kings (Matt 19:16–26). To be honest, we face the same temptations today as the rich young ruler. The good life of Western capitalism continues to be a significant hurdle and the attractions of Vanity Fair are an ongoing threat to a vibrant spiritual life.

One cannot be unimpressed with the initial quartet's immediacy in responding to the invitation of Jesus. How swift is their compliance: "Immediately, they left their nets," the writer notes, "Immediately they left the boat and their father" (Matt 4:20, 22). What courage, enthusiasm, and childlike spontaneity the disciples emanate. Such zeal often contrasts with our own lethargy, hesitancy, and lack of commitment. In fact, it raises the question of the nature of our own discipleship. Are we receiving in fullness the new vocation that Jesus is offering? Do we truly want to become "disciples" and "learners of Christ"? A constraint to a full-hearted "yes" is the danger of compartmentalizing our journey with Jesus. We give a cheerful affirmative in certain environments and hold back in others due to our own priorities and personal aspirations. Such a dichotomy keeps us from the power of "willing one thing" which Kierkegaard encouraged even in a less hectic age.[3] The strength of our faith builds as we assert it in every part of our lives; conversely, it diminishes when we suppress it, even when such inhibitions seem reasonable. Jesus's commendation of Mary who "chose the better part" by remaining an attentive disciple (despite the consternation of her sister Martha!) is a gainful reminder of the importance of reaffirming our "yes," no matter what pressures we face at the moment (Luke 10:42).

---

2. Bonhoeffer, *Cost of Discipleship*, 99.
3. Kierkegaard, *Purity of Heart*, 3.

Part I: Casting the Vision
Engaging the Great Work

Jesus not only invites his new friends to accompany him, he also challenges them with an entirely new type of fishing: "fishing for people" (Matt 4:19). His invitation is to a more profound calling than their seafaring trade. Now they will join him directly in the work of incarnating the kingdom of heaven on earth. There is a desire in all of us to do something with meaning and purpose, something deeper than our normal nine-to-five work. We want to contribute to a cause that is bigger than us. I remember my father waxing eloquently about the spirit of the Belfast people during the Nazi bombing runs. It went something like this: "We felt connected. As a people we took a great stand against the enemy and our blood ran with courage and zeal. After the war ended, it all settled back down; we missed the enemy we once faced." It is this type of focused, energizing work that Jesus invites his disciples to engage in. He also invites us on a similar mission—to take up our part in God's great work on planet Earth. This work in our specific sphere of influence is a work which only we can do. May we take it up with enthusiasm and gratitude because Jesus has deemed us fit to join the ultimate cause.

The Evangelist goes on to identify what the "fishing" of Jesus involves. It comprises three dimensions: teaching, proclaiming, and healing (or curing) (4:23). It is notable that Matthew begins with the importance of teaching, even more so than the performance of wondrous miracles. He reports that Jesus goes first to the synagogues (as Paul the apostle does later) to share with the congregants the deeper teachings of the Scriptures. The desire is that the people of Israel become true disciples and learners of God. We observe the same emphasis in the Gospel of Mark when the crowds are amazed at the power and authority of his teaching, saying, "What is this? A new teaching—with authority!" (Mark 1:27). This is not surprising. Jesus knows the ways of the Godhead more than any other individual and he feels compelled to communicate these mysteries to everyone. Curiously, this point is emphasized to his own cousin John when he has doubts about Jesus's messiahship. Jesus says to John's disciples, "Go and tell John what you hear and see: the blind receive their sight, the lame walk, the lepers are cleansed, the deaf hear, the dead are raised, and the poor have good news brought to them" (Matt 11:4–5). His focus is on "hearing" and receiving the word of God with power, before mentioning "seeing" the miracles of God.

Equally, receiving Jesus's word and delivering it to others becomes a keystone in the work of "fishing for people." The significance of Jesus's words can be seen when teachers of the Bible across our lands share God's word and the eyes of listeners light up in wonder and recognition. As we take up the mantle of sharing Jesus's words, so the ranks of God's kingdom increase and the Seer's song is fulfilled: "The kingdom of the world has become the kingdom of our Lord and of his Messiah, and he will reign for ever and ever" (Rev 11:15).

Proclaiming the Good News

The second dimension of "fishing" that Jesus annunciates is "proclaiming the good news [of the Kingdom]" (Matt 4:23). It points to our participation in sharing with those in our own spheres of influence the *kerygma*, the significance of Jesus's person and work. We routinely talk about what excites us. It is the same with telling the stories of Jesus. If he excites us, then let's pass it on so that others might also enjoy the gift of life. The Gospel is good news—not bad news! We have nothing to hold us back except our own pride. I remember my Uncle Charlie who spent his career in the British Navy, including seven years in India, visiting us in Toronto when I was a young lad. He had experienced a rich and full life but it all paled in his mind when he turned to Jesus in his mid-sixties. From that day on he had a constant smile on his face and the words of Jesus constantly on his lips. A musician friend of mine wrote a song called "My Lips and My Soul Sing Jesus." When I think of his song, I think of my Uncle Charlie joyfully praising God in the autumn years of his life! As disciples of Jesus we are invited to proclaim the good news of Jesus in the everyday of our lives. It doesn't involve being preachy or holier-than-thou; it simply means allowing our true selves to shine so that the light of Jesus is seen wherever we find ourselves.

The challenge we face is that we live in an age where bad news is more popular than good news. Bad news is the realm of mass media because it sells. People are attracted to stories of death, violence, murder, sex, power, war, and politics. These are the narratives which fill our news sources because they excite us and get our adrenalin going. Bob Dylan puts it well when he says,

> Good news in today's world is like a fugitive, treated like a hoodlum and put on the run. Castigated. All we see is good-for-nothing news. And we have to thank the media industry for that. It stirs

us up. Gossip and dirty laundry. Dark news that depresses and horrifies you.[4]

Good news is countercultural. It sounds out of place like it doesn't belong. Hence, there is a greater need than ever to announce the good news of Jesus. Now we have a *kairos* opportunity to speak the prophetic message of love. It is as if we are living in a black hole where the message of goodness is being sucked back into the abyss of darkness. We must keep speaking good news or it will be lost and the famine of muted silence will reign as our steady state of reality. The time is now for telling the truth of glad tidings for it will surprise the listener with its audacity and it just might be that attentive ears will hear it and spiritless lives will come to life.

The third part of our new vocation as lived out by Jesus is the work of "curing or healing" (Matt 4:23). Matthew tells us that people came from all over the greater region so that Jesus might touch them and make them well. When they came, he did not turn any of them away, healing them all. All were received, regardless of creed, gender, nationality, or defilement. As followers today, we also have this wholistic mission of word and deed, to be both evangelistic and prophetic—to back up our words with compassionate actions so that the impact of Christ is readily seen. A secular culture demands evidence—a degree of relevance—for the words of life to be considered in a skeptical age. One area that has resonance in our day is to take up the cause of the oppressed and the poor. Howard Snyder encourages the faith community to pursue this direction:

> God's people are called to defend the cause of the poor and needy within each nation and worldwide. The treatment of the poor, the needy and 'those who have no social power' becomes a test of the justness of any society or political system. Therefore, when the church works in behalf of the poor it is meeting specific human need and it is making a politically significant contribution.[5]

People often want to help but don't know how, so churches modeling in this area can be useful in giving others an opportunity to join in.

As I work on this chapter there are protests going on around the world on behalf of George Floyd, a black man who was brutally killed in the city of Minneapolis. This man was taken down by police for an alleged nonviolent crime and suffocated to death from officers' combined weight on

---

4. Douglas Brinkley, "Bob Dylan Has a Lot on His Mind."
5. Snyder, *Community of the King*, 114.

his neck and chest. Floyd was held down in a prone position for a total of eight minutes and forty-six seconds in spite of his recurring cries, "I cannot breathe"! The entire debacle videoed by several spectators has resulted in tens of thousands marching and protesting, proclaiming the mantra that "Black Lives Matter" in an effort to bring about some measure of justice for the execution of George Floyd. People of all walks of life have declared this abhorrent pattern of prejudice, hatred, and brutality against black men and women has been going on for too long and must be stopped.

This tragic state of affairs was first raised in my own consciousness as a young lad when our pastor Dr. Harry Faught traveled from Toronto to Selma, Alabama, in 1965, to march with Dr. Martin Luther King, protesting the lack of voting rights for African Americans. To our chagrin, here we are fifty-five years later and the same kind of inequality and oppressive hatred is still being experienced by our Black brothers and sisters. How slow we are to exchange our engrained patterns of prejudice for the boundless love of Christ which shows no trace of partiality (Rom 2:11).

Now the point at hand is that the church of Christ has a responsibility to stand up and raise its voice on behalf of the oppressed, which, in this case, is the repression of people of color by those in the power positions (normally white men). When the church speaks on behalf of marginalized and aggrieved peoples it acts in the spirit of Jesus and proclaims the values of the kingdom of God (Luke 4:18–19). This is what my pastor did those many years ago, and I am inspired by his modeling.

If we remain silent, we align ourselves with the powers of domination, and wittingly or unwittingly become players in the oppression of individuals and people groups who are created in the image and likeness of God. The teachings and example of Christ are crystal clear in this regard. They propel us to stand with the oppressed regardless of the inconvenience or fallout we may experience from doing the right thing.

This prophetic dimension of making a difference in our communities reinforces our words concerning Jesus's love. The Epistle of James makes it clear: "Religion that is pure and undefiled before God, the Father, is this: to care for orphans and widows in their distress" (Jas 1:27); again, "If a brother or sister is naked and lacks daily food, and one of you says to them, 'Go in peace; keep warm and eat your fill,' and yet you do not supply their bodily needs, what is the good of that? So faith by itself, if it has no works, is dead" (2:14–17). Compassionate charity must back up our voice of evangelism.

Part I: Casting the Vision

When we do so, the healing touch of Jesus is experienced as we walk with people in the here and now of their daily sojourn.

To this end it is helpful to reflect upon the sources that are shaping our conversation and conduct as we live out our journey of faith. Two salient questions aid our thinking: Who are we listening to? and Whose interests are we representing?[6] Our immersion in the online culture clouds our ability to think clearly and to own our own answers. We often simply parrot the pundits on our favorite news feed and bypass the hard work of personal contemplation. As believers there is an urgency to prayerfully consider what Jesus is calling us to and not be swayed by charismatic personalities, whether they be politicians, celebrities, or media hosts. When word and deed come together, the powerful witness of Jesus's enlivening presence is known, for in it "the kingdom of heaven has [truly] come near" (Matt 4:17).

Going Over the Wall

We began our reflection with a diving story from Little Cayman with the invitation to go over the top of Bloody Bay Wall and plummet deep into the mysteries of the coral reef. When we receive these initial commands of "repent" and "follow me," we are hearing Jesus's first words as he commences his public ministry. This is where it all begins. He invites us to accompany him on an adventure which opens up exciting new possibilities—both in the here and now and for every coming season of our lives. Richard Rohr points to this exhilarating journey as learning from past loves and embracing God's extravagant love, as he writes, "God seems to be 'turning' our loves around (in Greek, *metanoia*), and using them toward the Great Love that is their true object. All lesser loves are training wheels, which are good in themselves, but still training wheels."[7] All the other passions we have known point us in the direction of God's First Love—love for family, friends, music, sports, mountains, oceans, forests, plains, the arts—everything we enjoy comes from him, and through it all, he draws us, saying, "Come to me. Follow me. I am the essence of what your heart truly desires." Over and over, God reaffirms his love by inviting us to join his party, celebrate our union with him, and express gratitude for the blessings he has showered upon us. The invitation is proffered anew as Jesus encourages us

---

6. See Abraham, "Theological Response to the Ecological Crisis," 52.
7. Rohr, *Falling Upward*, 61.

to join his band of followers and participate in the great work of creating a new humanity of God.

Questions for Reflection:

1. As you consider your own faith journey, what are the areas that continue to come up in giving things over to God? What does the process of repentance look like in your life? Take some time to reflect on your journey of repentance and then journal about it to help gain clarity concerning next steps.

2. What fears come up for you as you consider launching out into the deep with Jesus? They might include your fear of how others view you if you take your walk with Jesus more seriously. You may have fears of loss—of friends, of opportunities, of experiences, of things you do not want to give up. Write down the nature of your fears and share them with Jesus as you wait upon the Spirit's leading.

3. As we have seen, a significant part of Jesus's ministry was his commitment to teach others about the values of the kingdom of God. As you consider your own faith community, is there a younger believer you could come alongside to nurture in the faith? Spend some time praying about this person and consider the key steps in bringing it to fruition.

Part I: Casting the Vision

4. Identify in your own sphere of influence how you can become a peacemaker. What practical ways can you engage to be a force for freedom, equal rights, and justice-making? Spend time reflecting upon prophetic texts like Micah 6:8, Amos 5:21–24, Hosea 12:6 and consider how you might become, as Saint Francis says, "an instrument of peace."

Chapter 2

The Lightness of Being

Laying Down One's Burdens

The present moment is always overflowing with immeasurable riches, far more than you are able to hold. Your faith will measure it out to you: as you believe, so you will receive.... Every moment the will of God is stretched out before us like a vast ocean which the desires of our hearts can never empty, but more and more of it will be ours as our souls grow in faith, in trust and in love.

JEAN-PIERRE DE CAUSSADE

Abandonment to Divine Providence, **41**

> *At that time Jesus said, "I thank you, Father, Lord of heaven and earth, because you have hidden these things from the wise and the intelligent and have revealed them to infants; yes, Father, for such was your gracious will. All things have been handed over to me by my Father; and no one knows the Son except the Father, and no one knows the Father except the Son and to anyone to whom the Son chooses to reveal him.*
>
> *"Come to me, all you that are weary and are carrying heavy burdens, and I will give you rest. Take my yoke upon you, and learn from me; for I am gentle and humble in heart, and you will find rest for your souls. For my yoke is easy, and my burden is light." (Matt 11:25–30)*

Part I: Casting the Vision

Jesus invites us to follow after him and make him the center of our lives. He offers us a new and powerful vocation to become his disciples, enter his school of discipleship, and work for goodness in the midst of a hurting world. The challenge we face is that we carry with us our share of brokenness and wounds. We follow after Jesus, but we bring baggage, tension, and pain. We do not come with a clean slate. For this reason, Jesus invites us to not only follow after him, but to *come to him*. He invites us to locate our solace, comfort, and maturation *in him*, and to draw strength from his bottomless well of love. The prophet Isaiah speaks of turning to the divine source and in it finding solace: "Those who wait for the Lord shall renew their strength, they shall mount up with wings like eagles, they shall run and not be weary, they shall walk and not faint" (40:31). It is in this spirit that we not only follow after Jesus, but come to him, and experience his consolation, equilibrium, and rest.

Eavesdropping on Jesus's Prayer

The preacher from Galilee prefaces his invitation to follow by offering a prayer to the Father which we overhear through Matthew's storytelling abilities. The prayer begins with the adoration of the Lord of heaven and earth who graciously responds to the poor and humble of heart rather than the erudite of the land who trust in their own wisdom. These Gospel words resonate with the lowly, the marginalized, and those lacking in power or riches. This refrain rings forcefully in the words of Mary's Magnificat, "He has shown strength with his arm; he has scattered the proud in the thoughts of their hearts. He has brought down the powerful from their thrones, and lifted up the lowly; he has filled the hungry with good things, and sent the rich away empty" (Luke 1:51–53).

Those who are powerful in the world's eyes do not feel any necessity for the divine reality. They are able to care for themselves by writing a check, employing hired help, or requesting others to do their bidding. Matthew depicts such attitudes not only in the actions of the rich but also in the predilections of the Pharisees and scribes. The PhDs of the day do not respect this humble Galilean because he lacks the education of the best schools. As a result, they arbitrarily reject his teachings. In contrast, those who are in need and unable to rely upon their own resources are the ones with receptive hearts who turn to God. The ones who have uncluttered and open hearts hear his words of life and are hungry to receive more.

Embedded in Jesus's prayer is also an instructive illustration of his own relationship with the Father. It is the dynamic of a father and son who walk in true intimacy. Jesus acknowledges that no one understands him as the Father does. It is not even close! His Father knows his thoughts and words even before he announces them. And vice versa. Jesus knows the deep currents of his Father's heart before any words are uttered. There is a profound interchange between the two which enables Jesus to overcome the negativity of many in his traditional Eastern culture. The good news for us is that through Jesus we perceive the heart of the Father. No one else reveals the Father's heart in such a clear and insightful manner. The British evangelist Michael Green exclaims, "If you want to know what God is like, look at Jesus. If you want to get through to God, come to Jesus. If you want to discover the epicenter of God's self-disclosure, you will find it in Jesus."[1] As a result, we are able to go to Jesus in confidence knowing that through him we are drawing close to the compassionate presence of our loving Abba.

Of course, more is being acknowledged in this prayer than simply a comparison to a well-working father-son relationship. Jesus is not simply a son. Rather, he is the true Son of the living God. In Jesus's prayer, we are overhearing the inner conversation of the Divine Family and are receiving a glimpse into the interior workings of the Godhead. As Jesus makes clear, "No one knows the Son except the Father, and no one knows the Father except the Son" (Matt 11:7). Similarly, John the Evangelist affirms this unique relationship in the words of Jesus, "The Father and I are one" and "The Father knows me and I know the Father" (John 10:30, 15). The knowledge which the Gospel writers address is not merely an intellectual understanding but speaks to an existential awareness within the inner movements of the Holy Trinity. Jesus knows all about the Father because he is in deep communion with him at a fundamental level.

As a result, as we come to Jesus, we are coming home to the Father, as Jesus portrays in the parable of the prodigal son returning home to his loving father. The act of coming home parallels the idea of repentance we saw in the previous chapter and a crucial step in the human-divine equation. "Like the turning of a key in a lock, it is the prelude to a new action . . . through which the light of the coming Day shines clear and transparent," muses the theologian Karl Barth.[2]

---

1. Green, *Message of Matthew*, 142.
2. Barth, *Epistle to the Romans*, 437. See also Buber, "Writings of Martin Buber, I and

PART I: CASTING THE VISION

Coming to the Master

With loving eyes Jesus looks at his prospective students and offers an invitation of welcome: "Come to me with all of your brokenness and pain." He understands that they—that we—are fragile and full of hang-ups, frustrations, self-doubt, and pain. Yet he invites us to bring it all and come. It is an honest invitation. Bring all of your garbage, all of your burdens, all of your psychological complexes, and give them to me and I will give you "rest" (note his emphasis in verses 28 and 29 as he repeats the word). In exchange for your interior restlessness, I will give you peace, confidence, and joy.

In his offer Jesus draws upon the Old Testament understanding of the word *shalom* which is normally translated as "peace." Here it does not refer to peace simply as an absence of violence but to a wholistic sense of well-being: *Shalom* in every corner of one's existence. Not "rest" as a state of inaction, but a sense of equilibrium, satisfaction, and abundance. In Jesus's overture we hear the echoes of the prophet Jeremiah mentioned earlier which sounds through the centuries: "Thus says the Lord: Stand at the crossroads, and look, and ask for the ancient paths, where the good way lies, and walk in it, and find rest for your souls" (Jer 6:16).

Experiencing *shalom* is clarified in the followup to Jesus's imperatives "Come" (*deute*) and "Take my yoke upon you and learn from me." The invitation is a beckoning to draw close and to pair your life with him even as oxen pair up to do the heavy lifting. Such a call is one that flows out of the workshop of Jesus. As a carpenter he would have fashioned such harnesses plenty of times for neighboring farmers who used them to prepare their fields. I wonder what Jesus was meditating upon as he carved, planed, and sanded the wood to form a well-fitting yoke? Perhaps he was thinking of the qualities of the farmer, his family, his children, his parents—all these kind folks he knew so well who would benefit from this tool he was shaping. The one who wanted the yoke had come to him, so he must do his best to meet his needs. One thing for sure, the initiative must come from the user, not the designer, as noted by one writer, "One comes to the person who has the yoke in order to put it on."[3] The motivation for putting on the yoke must come from us.

If we are to follow Jesus we are not to walk at a distance but are to travel closely, leaning and drawing strength from him in the everyday of

---

Thou."

3. Nolland, *The Gospel of Matthew*, 477.

our lives. Is this why we often do not accept the invitation to enter his rest? We prefer to be free from obligation. We do not want to be beholden to anyone. We prefer to go our own way even if it means experiencing deep pain. Ironically, we cling to our own hurt rather than pair up with Jesus who we fear will hamper our choices. Little do we know that Jesus only wishes the best for us and desires that we experience unfettered joy and happiness.

As we come to Jesus and walk with him the process of learning begins to deepen. It is interesting to note that the verb "to learn" (*manthano*) shares the same etymology as the noun "disciple" (*mathetes*), so that as we learn of Jesus, we become more and more his disciple. We are on a journey of becoming an apprentice of Christ; indeed, we might say that we are in the master's workshop learning the trade of our Master. This is not surprising, as we learn many things in life through imitation and observation. One on one, we watch, listen and learn, from teachers and mentors. In my own journey as a musician this has certainly been the case: hours and hours of tutelage, I have sought mastery of a craft in playing the guitar and in composing songs. It is the same as we walk with Jesus. We sit with him in silence, listening for his voice. We study the Scriptures to know his guidance. And we converse with him throughout the day to discern the Spirit's leading. It is a pilgrimage of intimacy and love, leaning on Jesus every step of the way.

A Gentle and Humble Teacher

Our Master is a gentle and humble teacher. He does not lord it over us but comes to us as a humble shepherd. In an age where humility is often seen as a disparaging quality, Jesus embraces it as a characteristic which represents the Father, whom he reveals to be our loving Abba. He comes to us in the person of the gentle Galilean, and through him demonstrates his respectful, tender, and compassionate ways. He does not force himself upon us. Rather, he gives us the opportunity to draw close or move away. He understands that our confidence in him takes time to develop, so he is patient and gives us all the time we need. He waits and waits and waits. He is always ready to hear our calls, and as we do so, he quickly responds. This is not inconceivable, as we ourselves respond to our own children's requests. How much more does Jesus and our heavenly Father understand our frailties and continue to offer their loving succor towards us.

Jesus's invitation "to come" and "to yoke with him" concludes with the two descriptors "easy" and "light." What we may view as ominous Jesus describes as "easy"—not "easy" as undemanding, rather, "easy" because it is the way that leads to true fulfillment and repose. Here Jesus employs a homonym—two words with similar spellings and soundings, but with significantly different meanings. In his language, "easy" (*chrestos*) sounds like the Greek name for the Messiah (*Christos*), "the anointed one." Thus, the way of Jesus is *chrestos* (easy) because it is the way of Christ (*Christos*).

Furthermore, the way of Jesus is "light." It is no longer the way of a thousand rules, the Pharisees' path, where a person earns one's standing before a holy God. Rather, it is a way of compassionate love, trusting that one's acceptance is based on the benevolence and kindness of God. Jesus portrays this gracious heart of God in the parable of the great banquet in Luke's Gospel. In it those who are rich and powerful reject a neighbor's invitation to attend his party as they pursue their own agendas. In contrast, the poor, weak, and marginalized of the community are more than happy to attend his celebration and enjoy the sumptuousness of the banquet. The parable speaks to the truth that one does not earn a place at the table but simply opens one's arms and receives the gracious gifts of the host. The parable reveals the Father's heart who compassionately receives the supplicant individual who freely trusts in His graciousness and beneficence.

Learning from the Master Teacher

The dilemma we face is that part of us is drawn by Jesus's invitation to come and experience his rest but another part remains ambivalent. There is a deep hole in our hearts which continues to be restless. As Augustine famously observed, "Our hearts are restless until we find our rest in God." We are so filled with desires, hopes, aspirations, tensions, and conflicts, that restlessness is simply a part of our day-to-day experience. Consequently, God steps back. If he doesn't, we are overcome by his blinding presence and simply fall down in awe. The Father's intention is that our coming to him is not based upon fear but on having a heart of longing and love. It is a kindly invitation to know his consoling presence. He waits for us to announce our "yes" to his overtures of love. As a result, we must search for him with an ardent heart to find the love of our lives.

What do we make of this simultaneous longing for God while at the same time resisting his adjuration? In part, we need to recognize that dissatisfaction is a basic ingredient of the human condition. We are discontented because, as creatures made in the image of God, we have a deep-seated desire for intimacy with our Creator. We long for him, but in love he is presently veiled. As a result, we gloss over this profound longing by limiting our attention to lesser desires and needs—such as money, sex, power, and recognition—that distract us from the fundamental longing that we all carry. John of the Cross recognizes our predicament as he laments, "Where have you hidden, Beloved, and left me moaning? You fled like the stag after wounding me; I went out calling you, but you were gone" (Canticle 1:1).[4] We want intimacy with our Creator, but in not finding him, we turn to secondary things which mask our deeper desire for the Ultimate Reality.

Another part of the answer is to accept that the angst we carry is not necessarily a bad thing. Our restlessness comes from our desire as persons created in God's likeness to rest in the arms of our Eternal Shepherd. When we realize this, we can then place less pressure on secondary things to fill up the hole in our hearts and live more gently upon the earth. Surface realities, no matter how blissful, will not eradicate our desire for uniting with the Maker of our wondrous universe. We rush around, exchanging relationships, careers, locations, and communities, thinking that we can get things right if we solve the puzzle of our lives. We miss the basic truth that what is needed is resting in an authentic relationship with our heavenly Father. Exchanging and moving surface pieces around, no matter how precious they seem, will not satisfy our deep longing that only finds equanimity in the sheltering of our triune God.

As we gain clarity on this fundamental truth we are more apt to freely turn to Jesus on a daily basis, experiencing his compassionate presence throughout the ups and downs of our everyday. As Edward Farrell reminds us, "We are to keep feeding on Jesus who is our soul food," so that we keep filling up the well of our souls which the vicissitudes of life draw down.[5] "We are to will one thing," Kierkegaard insists, which is his way of saying to keep our focus sharply on our Ultimate Reality.[6] We do not want to be derailed by the challenges or dissatisfaction that we face at any given time. As we do this, Jesus whispers to us, "I am with you each step of the way, in the good times and the hard times, even when you do not feel my presence, I am with you. Do not be discouraged, and never, never give up! Keep

---

4. Kavanaugh, *Collected Works of St. John*, 471.
5. Farrell, *Banquets of Ordinary People*, 30.
6. Kierkegaard, *Purity of Heart*.

holding on! Keep looking to me!" As we hear Jesus's reassuring words, his rest becomes our rest, his consolation becomes our consolation, and his spirit of integration becomes our spirit of integration.

A second factor in the quality of our rest flows from having a teachable heart. Moses models such a perspective when he receives guidance from his father-in-law Jethro to share the leadership responsibilities of Israel with other capable leaders (Exod 18:14). As he receives Jethro's advice, his onerous workload is lessened and an effective team of leaders is established to lead the nation. Do we have a teachable heart which enables us to learn from Jesus? Are we hardening our hearts, resisting growth, so that fruitful change is impeded at every turn?

As a scuba diver, I find an instructive image for verdant growth in the vibrant orange and crimson barrel sponges found on coral reefs. These simple organisms are some of the oldest living creatures on the planet—some living for a thousand years—and grow by simply allowing the ocean currents with their nutrients to pass through them. As the currents flow from one side of the sponge to the other, the enriching foods are absorbed by the sponge creating continuous health and sustenance. It would do us well to learn from our undersea friends and to live in "sponge mode" and to keep receiving new things from God that fuel and enrich our spirits and minds.[7] When we are teachable, fresh insights through the spirit of Jesus draw us deeper into renewed life and maturity as disciples of Christ.

The converse, of course, is a sober warning: when we become encrusted with hard hearts, we reject the overtures of the Spirit and experience spiritual atrophy.

Apprentices in the School of Discipleship

The journey of apprenticeship to Christ is a process of lifelong learning—of "walking the line." We never master it all. We constantly learn new things of God, ourselves, and others by the Spirit of Jesus and through our interactions with our sisters and brothers in the faith. Such an irenic spirit is praised by the early monastics who speak of it as the virtue of docility. This prized quality refers to a humble spirit which is willing to learn from all persons and especially from those who hold contrary positions.

From my pastoral vantage point, I have seen such amiable peacemakers play essential roles in a faith community when division and strife are

---

7. See also Sims, *Blue Fishing* for a similar idea.

the spirit of the day. Their calm manner and generous hearts soften the hardened callouses that people hold as they battle for the high ground of theological correctness. There is a great need for copious measures of docility so that when challenges occur within the community of faith they can be rectified and the witness of the church is not hampered. Through it all, the love of Christ must be valued more than any competing virtue. Greater than our commitment for correct thinking about God, must be our commitment to love one another in God, regardless of subpar theological understanding or expression. As both Saint Peter and Saint Paul remind us, love is the crux of knowing and following Jesus: "Above all, maintain constant love for one another, for love covers a multitude of sins" (1 Pet 4:8) and "And now faith, hope, and love abide, these three; and the greatest of these is love" (1 Cor 13:13).

In sum, we rejoice that as disciples of Jesus we are invited to be on his team. We no longer concern ourselves with simply personal goals. We entertain a larger vision, a greater calling. We are members of his company and are instruments in his hands for the kingdom of God. His Spirit now fills us and gives us energy to follow him with zeal and purpose. As we do so, our lives imitate Jesus's passion. As God's power (*dynamis*) fills us with energy, we are enabled to embrace the vocation that he has given us to follow. Our lives matter! We have a cosmic genesis! We are called to represent God in our world so that he is magnified and others are drawn to his limitless love. Let us do so with reckless abandon as we breathe in his life with every breath we take. Karl Rahner hints at the robust energy of "walking the line": "Every possibility of life is still open, because we can still find God, still find more."[8] Amazingly, we are able to pursue an adventure from a position of repose, as we rest in the arms of our Beloved who loves us with an unbounded and infinite love.

---

8. Rahner, *Great Church Year*, 105.

Part I: Casting the Vision

Questions for Reflection:

1. We fill up our lives in the pursuit of many things which ultimately distract us from our essential purpose of knowing and experiencing God. As you reflect upon your journey of faith, name the areas of distraction that move you away from knowing God more. Spend some time journaling about these proclivities and consider what next steps might help you go forward with more focus and purpose.

2. Jesus offers us his presence of rest. Indeed, he describes it as a rest characterized by "ease" and "lightness." How do these descriptors resonate with your own desires for God? How might the rest, ease, and lightness of Jesus help you in your everyday experience at work, home, and in your personal relationships? Pray about your desire for rest and ask Jesus to help you experience more of his consoling peace.

3. Jesus invites us to take his yoke upon ourselves and pair our lives with him. The yoke is not meant to be a burden but as a way of sharing the burdens of life with Jesus. In your own journey of faith how have you experienced the yoke of Christ? In what ways has Christ's yoke been a comfort or help for you in your everyday experience? Take time to journal about how his presence assists you in getting through hard times.

4. Jesus describes himself as being "gentle and humble of heart." He is a caring friend who travels with us. He doesn't give up on us. He does not exchange us on a whim for other friends. He is loyal, kind, and steadfast in his attention. In your history with Jesus how have you known his compassionate presence? Construct a mind map on a sheet of paper showing how the characteristics of Jesus interface and support you in your daily sojourn.

Chapter 3

The Black Hole of Anxiety

God is love, a benevolent power, a gracious authority, not someone to be feared. Indeed, God is the last person we need to fear. Jesus came to rid us of fear. Virtually every theophany in the scriptures . . . begins with the words: "Do not be afraid!" What frightens us does not come from God.

Ronald Rolheiser

Wrestling with God, 71–72

Do not store up for yourselves treasures on earth, where moth and rust consume and where thieves break in and steal; but store up for yourselves treasure in heaven, where neither moth nor rust consumes and where thieves do not break in and steal. For where your treasure is, there your heart will be also.

The eye is the lamp of the body. So, if your eye is healthy, your whole body will be full of light, but if your eye is unhealthy, your whole body will be full of darkness. If then the light in you is darkness, how great is the darkness!

No one can serve two masters; for a slave will either hate the one and love the other, or be devoted to the one and despise the other. You cannot love God and wealth.

Therefore I tell you, do not worry about your life, what you will eat or what you will drink, or about your body, what you will wear, is not life more than food, and the body more than clothing? Look at the birds of the air, they neither sow nor reap nor gather into barns, yet your heavenly Father feeds them. Are you not of more value than they? And can any of you by worrying add a single hour to your span of life? And why do you worry about clothing? Consider the

> *lilies of the field, how they grow; they neither toil nor spin, yet I tell you, even Solomon in all his glory was not clothed like one of these. But if God so clothes the grass of the field, which is alive today and tomorrow is thrown into the oven, will he not much more clothe you—you of little faith? Therefore do not worry, saying, "What will we eat"? or "What will we drink"? or "What will we wear"? For it is the Gentiles who strive for all these things; and indeed your heavenly Father knows that you need all these things. But strive first for the kingdom of God and his righteousness, and all these things will be given to you as well.*
>
> *So do not worry about tomorrow, for tomorrow will bring worries of its own. Today's trouble is enough for today* (Matt 6:19–34)

Jesus calls us to follow him.
Jesus calls us to discern our true life-purpose.
Jesus calls us to discover the nature of genuine rest.

WHEN WE REFLECT ON these invitations, is it possible that our hearts skip a beat with a measure of excitement? Or is there an element of doubt as to whether life allows such solace? There are so many challenges and our everyday journey brings innumerable heartaches. We have concerns for our children's well-being, we have financial struggles, we have health difficulties. There are enervating relationships at work, proclivities to bad habits, and the burden of succeeding in a hard-hearted culture. We usually think that the answers to our problems come from having "more and more." Yet our real experience is that we live our day-to-day with "less and less."[1] The conundrum is that we want "more" and do not accept our "less." We seek "more, more, more," chasing the American or Canadian dream, trying to keep up with neighbors, colleagues, and friends. As a result, we are filled with a pervasive lack of fulfillment, low-grade levels of depression, and a burdensome existential angst.

Cognizant of this wearisome approach to life, Jesus calls for a timeout so we can reclaim a healthy perspective as we embrace the dynamics of a God-centered creation. We do not face life's challenges alone; we live under the hand of our heavenly Father who never forgets, forsakes, or rejects us. No doubt, our universe, governed by the unrelenting laws of physics, poses a demanding existence for emotionally and physically fragile human beings. Nevertheless, the *buena nueva* is that we face these tribulations under

---

1. Scott, "Manna and Mammon."

the loving hand of our caring Abba. As the writer of Ecclesiastes notes, "There is nothing better for mortals than to eat and drink, and find enjoyment in their toil. This also, I saw, is from the hand of God" (2:24). Hurdles come our way; yet God is a constant source of strength and provides us with the power to live as "overcomers." We can embrace trust, confidence, and freedom from anxiety as we walk the line in our tutelage from Jesus.

Treasure in Heaven (Matt 6:19–24)

In this portion of The Sermon on the Mount, which flows from Jesus's teaching on prayer and fasting, Jesus encourages his disciples not to focus on or be dissuaded by the power of riches. He begins his discourse with a negative command, which I paraphrase: "Do not treasure up treasures upon the earth which are eroded by physical elements and are vulnerable to ingenious thieves" (Matt 6:19). In other words, refrain from stockpiling and overvaluing your possessions—your clothing, tapestries, gold, silver, jewels, and excessive cash. Jesus's negative imperative serves as an invitation to reflect upon the nature of our true treasures. They may point to possessions and money, or from another sphere all together—travel, adventure, fame, or power. Wherever they may lie, the thrust of the Master's inquiry is to examine our fundamental desires.

Following the *via negativa*, Jesus continues his discourse with a positive imperative, again my paraphrase, which invites us "to treasure up our treasures in heaven where they cannot be ruined by the elements or stolen by thieves" (6:20). This emphatic assertion makes sense from Matthew's understanding of the coming kingdom of God. If our destiny is to become citizens of the new dominion, then preparing for it with an appropriate lifestyle and mindset makes abundant sense. Jesus acknowledges this very point, as he summarizes that our treasure is found in the exact place where our heart is centered (6:25), or as one writer aptly notes, "One's treasure tells the tale of one's heart."[2] The Master's observation stops us in our tracks. Regardless of our religious jargon, meritorious church attendance, or charitable contributions, the telling of the tale is centered in what does our heart treasure. Only we know the answer to this critical question, which for Jesus is an essential one. Jesus doubles down on the same point with a second metaphor as he references our eyes and the nature of our seeing (6:22–23). The argument is based upon the understanding of sight in the

2. Nolland, *Gospel of Matthew*, 299.

first century: The eye enables a person to see by being a source of light. The light flows from the eye to the object in view and rebounds back to the eye.[3] The inference follows that if the eye is "sound" or "healthy" then the whole body is full of light because it views life plenteously (6:22). However, if the eye is "unhealthy" or "dark," then one's whole way of seeing is covered in darkness, betraying a heart of selfishness and covetousness—what was popularly known as "the evil eye" in Jesus's day.

At the same time, Matthew's fundamental point is that one's viewpoint is distorted by the evil emanating from one's heart. Certainly, we can think of the power of lust which is fueled by visual desire as evidenced in pornography and the urge to possess things as propagated by consumerism. Both of these realities run unchecked in contemporary society, even including the culture of the Western church. As a result, it is essential for us to hear the instruction of our Master Teacher and examine the nature of our seeing. In a society dominated by "screen time," it behooves us to be wise concerning the nature of our seeing so that we are able to work out Paul's directive, "Don't let the world around you squeeze you into its own mould, but let God re-mould your minds from within" (Rom 12:2, Phillips).

Jesus's cautions move beyond the nature of seeing, whether in light or in darkness. He does so by probing one's basic attitude toward money. He begins by saying what should be obvious: It is impossible to serve two masters. We end up loving one, while hating the other! Similarly, it is impossible to serve both God and wealth (6:24). The word Jesus employs for "wealth" is the Aramaic word "mammon" which is not limited to money, but includes all of one's riches. Mammon frequently has a negative nuance as it quickly morphs into an idol and an ultimate priority (Luke 16:9, 11). Jesus understands all too well that we are preoccupied with money and knows that we are infatuated with material things.

While wealth can be a tool for the kingdom of God, as Paul writes to Timothy (1 Tim 6:17–19), it contains its own danger. Paul points out that one's "love of money" can spread like a contagious virus and quickly rise up as a competing God (1 Tim 6:9–10). The great English poet Milton understood the lurking power of wealth as he imaginatively personified Mammon in *Paradise Lost* as

> the least erected Spirit that fell
> From Heav'n, for ev'n in Heav'n his looks and thoughts
> Were always downward bent, admiring more

---

3. Nolland, *Gospel of Matthew*, 301.

> The riches of Heav'n's pavement, trodd'n gold,
> Than aught divine or holy.⁴

Mammon has to do with our priorities and the choices we make. What are we going after in life? What are we truly pursuing? If we are committing ourselves to the kingdom of God, then our commitment to wealth has an impact on how we live our days. Is there not an uneasy tension in our cultural preoccupation with our investments—ironically called "wealth management"?⁵ The pertinent question for us is "Who are we going to serve?" We constantly need to question our relationship to our wealth—our possessions, our "stuff."

Turning from Anxiety (Matt 6:25–32)

Jesus, of course, knows all about the flip side of our preoccupation with money. He knows the human propensity for anxiety, and he understands that one of its many causes has to do with money. Do I have enough? Can I take care of my family? How much money do I need to do all of the things I want—even need—to do? These questions make us anxious and become a source for sleepless nights. Furthermore, such worries suggest that we do not grasp the reality of God's kingdom and that we are stuck in the system of mercantile dis-ease.

Jesus faces our anxiety head on and offers us some challenging words, "Therefore I tell you, do not worry about your life, what you will eat or what you will drink, or about your body, what you will wear. Is not life more than food, and the body more than clothing?" (6:25). He directs our attention to the world of nature and God's provision for his creatures. First, consider the birds of the air, and recognize that they do not worry about their food, but simply go about their business and God feeds them (6:26). Using the argument "from the lesser to the greater," Jesus turns and asks his disciples, "Are you not of more value than they?" The answer he is hoping to hear is the enthusiastic response, "Yes, if God provides for the birds of the air then surely he will take care of us who are created in his image."

Jesus introduces a second image as he encourages his disciples to "consider the lilies of the field" (6:28). Pointing at the surrounding flowers on the hillside, Jesus says that they are clothed with greater splendor than

---

4. John Milton, *Paradise Lost*, 1.678–83.
5. Bob Dylan in his song "Gotta Serve Somebody" alludes to the same idea of choices.

Israel's King Solomon ever experienced with his ornate robes. And to emphasize his point, he uses the compound verb *katamanthano*, or "consider," which employs the root of the noun "disciple" and the verb "to learn." Here Jesus is encouraging his disciples "to look, really look at, to examine with care" how God is truly Jehovah Jireh for all of his creatures. In truth, we are called to meditate on the wondrous provision of God and observe his sovereign handiwork in providing for all of creation. As the psalmist declares,

> You visit the earth and water it, you greatly enrich it; the river of God is full of water; you provide the people with grain, for so you have prepared it. You water its furrows abundantly, settling its ridges, softening it with showers, and blessing its growth. You crown the year with your bounty; your wagon tracks overflow with richness. (Ps 65:9–11)

Jesus then reminds his listeners who—and whose—they are. The "pagans" (the nations) are the ones who give themselves to such burdensome anxiety. They live within a worldview with gods who are capricious, self-serving, and undependable. It is not surprising that there is plenty of room for anxiety for them! One has to fight every battle on his or her own and any hope for divine assistance is simply wishful thinking. But this is not our situation as followers of Jesus. We have a Father in heaven who holds us in the palm of his hand and graciously provides for our every need. Indeed, through Jesus we have a compassionate Abba who knows our every need and who provides for everything we ask in Jesus's name.

Of course, by referencing the two creation images of the "birds of the air" and "the lilies of the field" Jesus does not encourage an attitude of irresponsibility. Nevertheless, he knows that anxiety narrows our field of view so that we are preoccupied by it and miss out on the wider blessings of life. Disquiet takes over and everything else is forgotten. Ceaseless restlessness becomes our habitual disposition underlining our inveterate need for control. The pithy platitude "to have all of our ducks in a row" reminds us of our efforts to manage every possible outcome through a hyper-degree of oversight. In light of this proclivity it is no wonder that Jesus sighs over his disciples' immature faith (Matt 6:30). Our desire for control dispels any need for trust as we attempt to straighten every turn in the road. No matter how we rationalize our approach, the outcome is the same: We live as "pagans," regardless of our religious platitudes.

The dual thrust upon money and anxiety is abundantly obvious in our sojourn through the COVID-19 pandemic. For the past year the entire world has struggled with a health and economic crisis due to a shrouded and deadly virus. As a result, people are concerned about both their physical and financial wellbeing. On top of this dual challenge there is the combined stress of isolation, loneliness, and the fear of the unknown. In our own strength we feel overwhelmed and inadequate to meet the collective strains of COVID-19. How do we overcome such worrisome hearts? Matthew's encouragement with his report of Jesus's words to release our anxiety is still relevant. We need to replace our myopic concentration on the problem at hand with a view of the greater horizon of hope and blessing that shines forth from the luminescent hand of our loving Abba.

We want to draw back into a living relationship with the Father which Jesus highlighted in the Lord's Prayer. We go to Abba in confidence with open hands and receive "our daily bread." We engage a relationship of intimacy and dependence with our loving and compassionate heavenly Father. We are not to try to do it all on our own as the mantra of our age repeats. Instead, each day we are invited to go to God and receive from him all that is necessary to live a happy and fruitful life—even in COVID times! This happens as we pay attention, live with awareness, and rely on our Father in a spirit of trust and living faith.

In the thirteenth century Saint Francis made this radical dependence on God the center of his Franciscan Order. The monks were to live as persons of faith and model this attitude as they performed works of service and "begged for alms," receiving provision for their sustenance. Saint Francis emphasized this directive because he insisted that those living under his order would not push God into the background through an excessive commitment to management and control.[6] Such a resolution to trust and faith in God's care continues to be an essential component of our journey of faith and life of discipleship. We are invited to learn how to be disciples (*katamanthano*), so that we are not controlled by a debilitating degree of trepidation which becomes an impediment for entering and enjoying the new kingdom of God.

Seeking First the Kingdom of God (Matt 6:33–34)

The key to overcoming anxiety is to maintain our focal point on our Creator God. As Jesus notes, "But strive first for the kingdom of God and his

---

6. See Bettenson, *Documents of the Christian Church*, 128–32, on the order of Saint Francis.

righteousness, and all these things will be given to you as well (Matt 6:33). Our top priority in life is to live in a dynamic relationship with the living God. Everything else is secondary to this primary directive. Before seeking money, possessions, security, or status, we are to know God and live a life that is pleasing to him. Greed of any sense—any form of idolatry—will distance us from "where the good way lies." Our preoccupations will narrow our field of vision and limit the degree of joy in our daily experience. These include our broodings upon our physical health and our pocketbook.

I was struck by the fleeting nature of wealth on a recent Bolivian outing to the country estate of The Tin King, Simón Iturri Patiño (ca. 1920s–40s). His circle of friends included Walt Disney and John Rockefeller, and at one point he was one of the richest individuals in the world.[7] Lamentably, his fortune was established on the backs of poor Bolivian workers who were paid a pittance while he and his family lived in luxury. He built opulent homes in Cochabamba and a villa in the countryside with luxurious gardens, exotic vegetation, and flowing fountains. He constructed mansions in the mining cities of Oruro and Potosi and in other South American cities including Bueno Aires. Greed—a desire for more—was his passion for living, all the while his workers suffered from poor pay and appalling working conditions. His single-minded focus on wealth went as far as manipulating government officials to have troops march against protesting miners at his Catavi mine, causing the loss of over four hundred lives.

The story of Patiño plays out eerily as in Jesus's parable of the plantation owner who builds several large barns to hoard his wealth so that he can pursue a sumptuous lifestyle (Luke 12:13–21). Unknowingly, the plantation owner's life ends abruptly and his great fortune is left behind. Jesus summarizes the parable with a shot across the bow to all who are addicted to wealth and power, "So it is with those who store up treasures for themselves but are not rich towards God" (12:21). Alas, I fear that Simón Patiño was a real-life exhibit of this sobering story.

Rather than obsessively seeking for more—more wealth, more possessions, more status, more power—flowing from a restless heart, we are encouraged to live one day at a time, trusting in the provision of our compassionate Father. We are invited to slow down and receive the day that God has given to us. We are encouraged to resist rolling around in the past or the future; rather to stay in the day, standing our ground, and "enjoy[ing]

---

7. In Malcolm Gladwell's "Outliers" the fortune of Patino was estimated to be 81.2 billion dollars—a total net worth greater than Bill Gates, Carlos Slim, or Warren Buffett.

the cosmic dance which is always there."[8] Jesus admonishes us to first seek the kingdom of God and the necessities of life will be given to us as well. We are not to live frenetic lives, consumed by anxiety, because Jehovah Jireh watches over his people, even as he did for the children of Israel. We can rest and trust in the beneficence of God. "Take delight in the Lord," the psalmist writes, "and he will give you the desires of your heart" (Ps 37:4). If this is the case, surely, God will provide for our fundamental needs, including shelter, food, drink, and clothing—even during a worldwide pandemic.

Ironically, what often keeps us from enjoying the present moment is our inveterate preoccupation with tomorrow. The Master Teacher recognizes this human proclivity and addresses it directly as he insists, "So do not worry about tomorrow, for tomorrow will bring worries of its own. Today's trouble is enough for today" (Matt 6:34). The God of tomorrow will take care of tomorrow, so stay present in the day, and receive it from God's hand. If we take time to think about it, there are numerous reasons why it is pointless to worry about the morrow, as pointed out by one observer: "We may be dead; what we fear may not happen; our preparations may match poorly the actual needs of tomorrow; we burden ourselves down (unnecessarily) with worry."[9] It really is useless to dwell on future exigencies. It simply is not productive.

The apostle Paul suggests a familiar alternative to our worries, words worth repeating often:

> Do not be anxious about anything, but in everything by prayer and supplication with thanksgiving, let your requests be made known to God. And the peace of God, which surpasses all understanding, will guard your hearts and your minds in Christ Jesus. (Phil 4:6–7)

As we follow the apostle's counsel, we return to the "one day at a time" focus of the Lord's Prayer, which is to stay with the day, live with awareness, and enjoy the ongoing presence of God's kingdom.

Walking the Line

The teaching of Jesus comes to us in the form of poetry, not prose. The references to the birds of the air and the lilies of the field are symbols—what

---

8. Merton, *New Seeds of Contemplation*, quoted in Boyle, *Tattoos on the Heart*, 166.
9. Nolland, *Gospel of Matthew*, 315.

Carretto calls "a parable of created things"[10]—used by Jesus to present a picture of trust and confidence in God. We are not to be preoccupied with the pursuit of wealth or the distractions of our possessions, but we are called to enter and receive the kingdom of God that flows from the river of his love. Such an invitation reminds us that it is necessary to pay attention to our attraction to mammon. We live in a consumerist age and face the lure of money, possessions, beautiful things, food, clothes, and drink. The marketing machine draws us into their purview to purchase cars, cell phones, iPads and computers, household furnishings, expensive clothes, and exotic vacations. This virtual bombardment tempts and derails us, eroding our passion for the kingdom of God.

So what practical steps can we take to move forward? A helpful first step is to review our actual spending habits. Such an exercise may reveal surprising insights as to how much money we spend on our physical needs as opposed to how much we give away for the work of God through his church or other compassionate agencies. This type of financial review is especially needed in our current environment as we are literally killing the earth through our greed and excessive lifestyle. There is an urgency to pause and reevaluate our financial practices for the good of the planet and the amelioration of those who are living on the margins of society.

A second consideration is to have a greater degree of awareness and compassion for those who are involuntarily poor. As the Lord's Prayer reminds us we are to pray for "*our* daily bread" and not simply "*my* own daily bread." Jesus switches to the first-person plural—"*our* daily bread," "*our* debts," "*our* debtors"—as he moves from addressing one's relationship with the Father (Matt 6:9–10) to articulating the petitions of the faith community (6:11–13). By this shift he is advocating for a compassionate and caring spirit for all of the families of the earth, as affirmed by the apostle Paul in the letter to the Ephesians: "For this reason I bow my knees before the Father, from whom every family in heaven and earth takes its name" (3:14–15). The invitation is to embrace our role as instruments of peace, reconciliation, and provision for all the peoples of the earth. It falls short if we simply focus on our own welfare at the expense of others who may not have enough to survive. As a result, we need to hear again the clarion call that Micah trumpets to the people of Israel: "He has told you, O mortal, what is good; and what does the Lord require of you but to do justice, and to love kindness, and to walk humbly with your God?" (Mic 6:8). This

---

10. Carretto, *God Who Comes*, 11.

appeal for compassion reminds us of the essential ministry of Jesus and his overtures for us to participate in the ministry of preaching, teaching, and healing (Matt 4:23–25), which we considered in chapter 1.

A third "So what?" for our deliberation is to welcome the power and love of our heavenly Father as Jesus emphasizes in his discourse. No longer are we to succumb to the spirit of cynicism and despair which prevails in our age. The mores of today's world push us in the direction of freneticism, materialism, and competition to attain some degree of recognition and success. But this is not how we are to live within the coming kingdom of God. Instead, we are to live as people of hope in a desperate and hopeless world. As Jesus announces in his invitation to come and experience rest, so we are to exchange our frantic busyness for a lifestyle that is characterized by sabbath rest. This practice of equanimity comes from having a confidence in God and a resolute intentionality to stay in the moment and not race into tomorrow's worries.

A helpful way to reinforce spiritual leisure is to engage the practice of gratitude on a daily basis. Brother Lawrence reminds us in *The Practice of the Presence of God* to do everything with an open and grateful heart: "That he was pleased when he could take up a straw from the ground for the love of God, seeking him only, and nothing else, not even his gifts."[11] His encouragement is to receive every day with gratitude with its individual moments—all of the pleasures that flow from God's throne—everything that communicates that all is grace and "all will be well."[12] We can develop a keen sense of awareness so that life's bounty does not go unnoticed. We can learn to appreciate and celebrate the largesse of God. As we live in this spirit, the cynicism, apathy, and malaise that weigh us down, give way to charity, delight, and tranquillity that flow from grateful hearts for the gifts of Abba's bounteous care.

Finally, Jesus's instruction encourages us to live with confidence as we travel our everyday in the presence of our loving God. A specific step that helps us in this regard is to give Jesus the little stressors that chip away at our experience of God's peace. All of us carry such stressors. A difficult neighbor who is a constant source of irritation. A worker on the line who intentionally mocks us for our faith. Insufficient income which keeps us on edge. Cutbacks in our work division which threaten our livelihood. Concern for our children and their struggles at school. A myriad of stressors

---

11. Foster and Smith, *Devotional Classics*, 83.
12. See Juliana of Norwich, *Revelations of Divine Love*, 130–32.

forces us into the world's mould of unrelenting anxiety and debilitating depression. We feel overwhelmed and emotionally paralyzed. To get unstuck we need to give Jesus the stressors that are hindering us. Whatever anxieties we face, let us turn them over to Jesus, so that we hear his consoling words, "Do not be anxious about tomorrow. Rather focus on the day that awaits you." As we do this, old patterns change. Negative messages of inadequacy and self-deprecation are replaced with positive ones of gratefulness and love. We unclench our fists, release our anxieties, and "walk the line" with the Master who leads us where "the good way lies."

Questions for Reflection:

1. Jesus's commandment "to strive first for the kingdom of God" continues to be a central injunction from our Master Teacher in our own day. In contrast, we hear so many messages in our wordy world drawing us to satiate our needs, wants, and desires. What areas of life draw you away from seeking God's will and substituting your own pursuits and endeavors? How might you begin the process of restoring a sense of spiritual equilibrium in your faith journey?

2. Anxiety is a bane of modern living. It seems almost impossible to calm our minds and spirits and regain a sense of peace. Yet, Jesus speaks a word of tranquility amidst the storms of life as he calmly announces, "Do not worry about your life, what you will eat or what you will

drink, or about your body, what you will wear" (Matt 6:25) and "your heavenly Father knows that you need all these things" (6:32). What spiritual disciplines help to fill up your interior well so that you are not overloaded with anxiety? How do you engage these practices in your everyday?

3. Brother Lawrence encourages us to practice the presence of God throughout our day. In your journal write down the specific exercises that assist you in staying conscious of God's comforting presence throughout your everyday. Such exercises as breath work, memorization of Scripture, repeating of scriptural phrases throughout the day, short arrow prayers of petition, daily quiet times, and daily communication with a soul friend may be of help.

4. It is a challenge to really understand one's spending patterns. Do a self-audit in terms of eating (groceries, takeout, restaurants), drink (coffees, wines, beers), clothing (shopping at stores, online), shelter (home improvements, furniture, appliances), travel/entertainment (vacations, travel, hobbies), benevolent giving (contributions to church, social and justice causes). Record your expenditures over a month and see what you learn. What changes might you make? What spiritual rewards come from those changes?

Chapter 4

The Enigma of the Downward Way

There is a necessary suffering that cannot be avoided, which Jesus calls "losing our very life," or losing what I and others call the "false self." Your false self is your role, title, and personal image that is largely a creation of your own mind and attachments. *It will and must die in exact correlation to how much you want the Real.*

Richard Rohr

Falling Upward, 85

From that time on, Jesus began to show his disciples that he must go to Jerusalem and undergo great suffering at the hands of the elders and chief priests and scribes, and be killed, and on the third day be raised. And Peter took him aside and began to rebuke him, saying, "God forbid it, Lord! This must never happen to you." But he turned and said to Peter, "Get behind me, Satan! You are a stumbling-block to me; for you are setting your mind not on divine things but on human things."

Then Jesus told his disciples, "If any want to become my followers, let them deny themselves and take up their cross and follow me. For those who want to save their life will lose it, and those who lose their life for my sake will find it. For what will it profit them if they gain the whole world but forfeit their life? Or what will they give in return for their life?

"For the Son of Man is to come with his angels in the glory of his Father, and then he will repay everyone for what has been done. Truly I tell you, there are some standing here who will not

Part I: Casting the Vision

taste death before they see the Son of Man coming in his kingdom."
(Matt 16:21–28)

A FEW YEARS AGO, I led a group of Tyndale University students to Israel to participate in a course called "History and Geography of the Holy Land" at Jerusalem University College. In our studies we traveled to significant sites throughout the country of Israel. At one stretch we found ourselves in Israel's far north, on the snowy slopes of Mount Herman, crossing over to Caesarea Philippi to the infamous Cave of Pan, which, at one time, housed the busts of various Greco-Roman gods. It is within these same environs that Jesus asks his disciples the cogent question concerning the nature of his identity, "Who do people say that the Son of Man is?" (Matt 16:13–16). It is a powerful scene to imagine the group contemplating his probing query while looking at the sculpted statutes of Pan, Echo, Hermes, and other Greek and Roman gods in the high stone niches. As the group ponders Jesus's question, slowly the answers begin to sound within the cave's chamber: "Some say you are John the Baptist"; others say, "Elijah"; "I've heard, Jeremiah"; a lot of people say you are "one of the prophets" (16:14). After the initial rush of responses, and a moment of silence, Jesus raises the singular question, "But who do you say that I am"? To everyone's amazement, Peter (as only Peter can) delivers the sterling answer, "You are the Messiah, the Son of the living God" (16:16). Hearing Peter's word, Jesus affirms his insight, "Peter, this insight was not yours alone but was prompted by our heavenly Father."

Curiously, following this revelatory acumen, Jesus predicts his own passion. Peter is horrified and brashly chastises Jesus for his pessimistic perspective! Upon hearing these words Jesus distances himself from Peter, rebuking him with the charge, "Get behind me, Satan! You are a stumbling-block to me; for you are setting your mind not on divine things but on human things" (16:23). No doubt, this leads to an uneasy, sustained silence amongst the group of disciples. Alas, community building is never easy, even if the leader is the Son of God!

On the heels of this heated moment, Jesus speaks directly and passionately to his burgeoning band of disciples about the nature of discipleship. These words—indeed, commands—lay out the costly nature of following Christ. It requires us to fully identify with him, not only in his glory, but also in his person as the suffering Messiah. The lesson he bids us to learn is not an easy one. It requires us to travel the road of suffering. And mysteriously, it ends with redemption and abundant life as we "walk the line" with Jesus.

Choosing Life

At first glance, the directives that Jesus delivers here to his disciples seem rather off-putting: "If any of you want to become my followers, let them deny themselves and take up their cross and follow me" (16:24). Strong words, for sure, but understandable, as we hear Jesus pressing potential disciples on the radical nature of discipleship. Previously he had spoken to his immediate band the upbeat words, "Come and follow me and I will make you fishers of men and women" (Matt 4:19). Here Jesus extends his call to a wider group of listeners who are contemplating the path of discipleship. Indeed, it is an ongoing summons which sounds across the generations—"if any of you want to become my followers." In hearing these words, we also receive the good news and an invitation to follow Jesus as his disciples. But it is a demanding way and Jesus wants us to weigh the cost carefully, not barging ahead without discerning the nature of the call.

Jesus's words comprise three separate imperatives: "deny," "take up your cross," and "follow." Denying oneself speaks to giving up our own interests for the cause of Jesus and for the greater good of others. This is a tall order, not something to be entered into lightly. If I am going to follow Jesus, his agenda becomes mine and his goals and kingdom are to transcend my own limited and self-centered interests. Wow! The imperative "deny yourself" certainly gets our attention whether for Jesus's immediate audience or for us two thousand years later. We aren't built to deny ourselves. Indeed, what we usually do is quite the opposite. We know what we want and we want it right away. We are not good at delaying our desire for gratification even when it makes a lot of sense. So, Jesus jumps right in, firing a cannon shot across our bow to get our attention.

The second command is even more demanding, as Jesus encourages the potential disciple to "take up your cross," an allusion to the Roman practice of condemned criminals carrying the crossbeam for their own crucifixion. Metaphorically, "bearing one's cross" speaks of identifying with the suffering of Jesus and sharing his compassionate journey with the poor and hurting of the world. Of course, no one really wants to suffer. But if we are going to align ourselves with Jesus, then we are called to "join with

Part I: Casting the Vision

him in the fellowship of his sufferings," even as Paul reminded the believers in Philippi (Phil 3:10). This process of identification is a demanding one which necessitates significant degrees of suffering. The inner person is refined and reshaped into the maturity of Christ's image. Surprisingly, suffering also becomes a way of renovation as life's challenges become opportunities or stepping stones to know God more fully and authentically.

With the third imperative, Jesus bids us to "follow him"—a command recorded in all four Gospels, suggesting its importance to the biblical record.[1] It is spoken here in the ongoing present tense which means that our degree of following Christ is to be continuous. We are not to start, then stop, and then pick it up again in the future when it is more convenient. No. Following Jesus is a steady-state phenomenon, an uninterrupted affirmation of declaring our "yes" to Christ through all the ups and downs of our faith journey. It is not just saying "yes" when we feel like it. But it is a radical call to obedience, which Bonhoeffer explains is an all-encompassing invitation "to come and die."[2]

Jesus elaborates on what it means to follow him, saying, "For those who want to save their life will lose it, and those who lose their life for my sake will find it" (Matt 16:25). To understand what the Master Teacher is alluding to we need to consider the nuances of the word "life" (*psyche*). At a basic level, of course, "life" speaks to our biological existence. Each of us expends enormous energy and expense to preserve that gift of physical life. Furthermore, our obsession with physical appearance and sexual desire often takes precedence over all other aspirations, demonstrating our preoccupation with our bodies. A second denotation for *psyche* is "existential life." Jesus uses the word in this sense when he assures his listeners, "Those who lose their life for my sake will find it" (16:25). Our physical life may be lost on account of following him, but our deeper, existential life continues unabated as we remain in relationship with Jesus.

Jesus clinches his argument: "What does it profit someone in gaining the entire world if it means losing your "existential life"? The question is rhetorical because the answer is painfully obvious: *nothing*! There is no good exchange for the value of our eternal souls! Everything else pales in comparison. In the Faustian myth, the scholarly Faust makes a pact with the devil to exchange his soul for a time of earthly success and achievement. His experience of great notoriety quickly loses its luster when Satan comes

---

1. See Mark 8:34—9:1; Luke 9:23–27; John 12:25 for the other accounts.
2. Bonhoeffer, *Cost of Discipleship*, 99.

knocking on his door to claim his prize and the temporal contract is seen for what it is—vanity and foolishness.

The Glory of the Cross

In Jesus's instruction here in Matthew's Gospel, there are two enigmatic truths that deserve further elaboration. First, when Jesus calls us to "deny ourselves," we actually improve our lot. How can this be? His command gains traction as we link it to the teaching of Saint Paul who exhorts us to "put off the old self" and to "put on the new self" (Col 3:9–10). Thomas Merton describes the apostle's idea as "clothing the false self" versus "clothing the true self" in his book *New Seeds of Contemplation*. We need to recognize the futility of pride and our desire to impress others with achievements, successes, or other self-centered attempts of "cloth[ing] the false self and construct[ing] its nothingness into something objectively real."[3] Such a fictitious self cannot last. It is ephemeral and has no reality. Instead, we are to exchange it for the true self which is created by God and is comprised of love, compassion, forgiveness, and deeds of mercy. This genuine self is weighty and is the only one that God knows and loves, ultimately entering into eternal bliss.

Second, the cross leads us to the triumph of resurrection. Jesus invites us to take up our cross, align ourselves with his path of suffering, and follow him through the death barrier into resurrection life. It is obvious that this path significantly contrasts with the world's paradigm of seeking glory while jettisoning suffering. We want glory, but we are also more than happy to leave the pain behind. Jesus understands that this approach is fool's gold, for the path of abundance must pass through the heart of suffering before it reaches the plenty of resurrection. This passageway is the same for all disciples, past and present, including Paul on the road to Damascus, when the resurrected Christ spoke to him from heaven and subsequently told Ananias, "how much he [Paul] must suffer for the sake of my name" (Acts 9:16). Every parent knows the truth of Jesus's words, as the joy of parenting is experienced amidst the path of much sacrificial love. Certainly, the path of conversion requires us to descend deep into our own pain if we are to transcend it and enter into the rest of Jesus. There is no other way. There are no shortcuts! We must all descend into our own hell to be liberated—to

---

3. See Merton, *New Seeds of Contemplation*, 33–36.

be freed from our demons by the power of Christ's Spirit. He sets us free, indeed.

The film *Dead Man Walking* presents this mystical descent in a powerful fashion as it tells the story of convicted killer Matthew Poncelet who is on death row at Louisiana State Penitentiary for the murder of a teenage couple. Due to his horrific crime and his surly attitude, he is treated badly by the prison staff and feels isolated in his own pain, guilt, and anger. The one person who treats him humanely and demonstrates a degree of solace is Sister Helen, who visits him regularly as he awaits his coming demise. Throughout his incarceration Matthew has denied the charge and blamed another prisoner for the death of the two young people. However, as his trust in Sister Helen grows, Matthew is finally and tearfully able to admit that he killed the boy and raped the girl. While being wheeled towards the execution room the film concludes with Sister Helen whispering in his ear, "Keep your eyes on me, and the last face you see, will be my face of love."

Matthew travels through his own self-made hell but ends his life in hopeful assurance with the sustenance of Sister Helen's compassionate love. It is a journey that, one way or the other, we all travel. Bear our cross. Carry our suffering. Rise to new life in the name of Jesus.

The Downward Way

The way of the cross means standing with those who are weak and marginalized by the "principalities and powers" of our age (Eph 6:10). It is hearing the words of Jesus to come and experience his rest and join with him in ameliorating the weighty burdens of the poor, the *anawim*. From the world's perspective, the downward way of identifying with the challenges and struggles of the poor is one of foolishness—a pointless loss of status and power. The world assumes that the increase of one's wealth with its attendant consequences is the consummate goal. From a spiritual perspective, the hoarding of wealth hardens one's heart and makes one insensitive to the needs of others.

In contrast, the descending path is counterintuitive. This misunderstood downward mobility ultimately leads us into a life-affirming pilgrimage of bearing fruit and an experience of abundance. The mystery of the kingdom is found in choosing the narrow and less-trodden path in which we step aside from the highway of competition and comparison and embrace the upside-down kingdom of Jesus's love. With such a mindset, the sacrificial words of the gospel make sense: "No one has greater love than this, to lay down one's life for one's friends. You are my friends if you do what I command you" (John 15:13–14). It is in the process of giving our lives away that we become friends with God's creation and instruments for healing and reconciliation.

To underline the importance of pursuing the downward path, Jesus introduces the word *praxis* (from which the English word "practice" is derived) when he emphasizes that "he will repay everyone for what has been done" (Matt 16:27). This is not a foreboding statement, but one of assurance. He recognizes our service and will reward us for our contribution "for what has been done" for God's kingdom"—our *praxis*. Here Jesus encourages the believer to nurture a "spiritual practice" of compassion and love. Christ charges us to replace a self-centered, egoistic mindset with an intentional lifestyle of radiating God's love, even as William Blake mused, "We are put on earth for a little space that we might learn to bear the beams of love."

In light of Jesus's pronouncement, we ask ourselves, "What is my spiritual practice and what does my way of life say to others?" Paul speaks to this same idea as he encourages the Roman church to "not be pressed into the world's mold but be transformed by the renewing of your mind" (Rom12:2, Phillips). Through this invitation the apostle urges us to develop a new way of thinking which is not focused on the mores of the world. We are to be aligned with the Holy Spirit, ushering in the compassionate fires of God's kingdom. As such, Christ exhorts us to step out of the world's parade which is characterized by a me-first attitude.

We live in a narcissistic age where personal desires often trump the needs of others. In theory, we may be concerned for others but in practice we focus on ourselves and our own family. It is all about our own needs, wishes, aspirations, and dreams. Everybody and everything else is secondary! As Jesus teaches in his parable of the Good Samaritan, are we like those who bypass the wounded individual while focusing on our own agenda? Or, do we interrupt our own plans to address the needs of others? Obviously, we are to imitate Jesus's mentorship of love, kindness, and generosity.

The award-winning film *Roma*, named after a *barrio* in Mexico City, tells the story of an upper-middle-class family in the process of disintegration due to the father abandoning his wife and children. The story focuses on their servant Cleo who loves the children as her own and protects them amidst the challenges the family is undergoing. During a failed attempt of a family vacation, Cleo is with the children at the beach while the mother is doing errands. While minding the smallest child, the other two are playing in the ocean waves and are caught up in a current taking them out to sea. Instantly, Cleo, a non-swimmer, enters the surf, going deeper and deeper. Her eyes are transfixed on the children, knowing that they are approaching the point of no return. With one final push she reaches the small children and carries them safely back to shore. As the mother returns, she finds them all exhausted at the water's edge, with the children crying that Cleo had rescued them from drowning.

The servant plays a Christ-figure as she risks her own life for the benefit of the family she loves. In stark contrast to the wayward father, Cleo represents a stunning rejection of the world's mores that seeks one's own advancement at the expense of others. Instead, she assumes the downward path so that the ones she loves might survive the storm of dissolution. It is this type of sacrificial love that Jesus looks for as he encourages his disciples to carry their own cross. Perhaps we can think of Jesus saying something like this: "I am looking for the Cleos of the world—people who actually care about the predicaments of others. If this is the kind of person you want to be, then step out of the world's parade and join me on the path that leads to abundant life." It is by taking up our cross and following Jesus that we become a bit more like Cleo, and less of the self-focused cronies we often resemble.

The Movement Towards Authenticity

When Jesus calls us to "take up our cross" he is not inviting us to sign up for a new form of asceticism, monasticism, or performance-based system for entering God's kingdom. Neither is he beckoning us to a path of diminishment which requires us to set aside our own sense of personhood. Rather, when Jesus speaks of picking up our cross, he is inviting us to engage a journey of self-discovery in order to find our true selves. It means moving away from the social customs of our culture shaped by competition, achievement, success, power, money, and celebrity status, and entering the downward way of love and compassion.

As Richard Rohr reminds us, embracing this path is a challenging prospect because we are a "first-half-of-life culture." By this he means that we largely focus on ourselves and *surviving successfully* and neglect "second-half-of-life movements" such as convergence, acceptance, and tolerance.[4] To this end, taking up our cross speaks of identifying with the life of Jesus, responding to his invitation, becoming a child of God, and practicing a lifestyle of compassion. It is not about being better than others, but as the theologian Paul Tillich enjoins, "accepting our acceptance" by a compassionate God who desires that we come to know our esteemed value as his beloved children.[5]

In the command to "take up our cross" we are encouraged to make our spiritual journey an everyday habit. It is to be an ongoing relationship whereby God "daily bears us up" (Ps 68:18–19) and we "look to him daily" (Ps 121). We are to go to God not just in challenging times, but every day, even as Adam and Eve met with God habitually in the garden of Eden. This spiritual practice ("praxis") is not an intellectual theory about an invisible God, but is meant to be a lived confession. It speaks to a living relationship, in which we imbibe the Spirit in every breath. There isn't a single aspect of life separated from our dynamic of knowing God. As we commit to this pattern of living, our principal purpose is not to gain first place at the expense of others (Phil 2:4), but to be instruments of God's love towards all of God's creation.

The symbol of the cross speaks to the nature of suffering and its role in the process of spiritual maturation. Embracing the cross is the antithesis of fleeing any degree of suffering that seems a pointless and intrusive interruption. The compassionate path, in contrast, recognizes the refining property of suffering within the process of spiritual transformation. As the apostle Peter writes, "In this you rejoice, even if now for a little while you have had to suffer various trials, so that the genuineness of your faith—being more precious than gold that, though perishable, is tested by fire—may be found to result in praise and glory and honor when Jesus Christ is revealed" (1 Pet 1:6–7). Further, the import of suffering is not only for our own benefit but is a help to others as we share in their suffering through a spirit of solidarity and familial love. To walk with those who are suffering in such a manner provides solace and creates a space for God's *shalom* to be experienced and known.

Living in this manner resonates with the heartbeat of God who gives himself away so that we might grow into the fullness of his love. Of course, from one side of the equation there is a cost in pursuing the way of compassion, as there is an aspect of diminishment in the actions of self-denial. On

---

4. Rohr, *Falling Upward*, xiii–xxix.
5. Tillich, *Courage to Be*, 160.

the other side—the most important side!—we receive God's blessing in the here and now, as we align ourselves with Jesus in the downward trajectory of the giving and receiving of compassionate love. It is in the act of emptying our hands that God fills them once again with the abundance of his extravagant self-giving.

A Story from the Parish

Compassionate love is amply demonstrated in our world as caregivers act sacrificially for the well-being of their children. I see this in my own faith community where grandparents take up the role as the primary nurturers in difficult situations. Compassionately they spread out their limited resources so that during hard times their loved ones have shelter, food, and access to education.

I think of Eleanor who lives in a four-story walk-up in the vicinity of our church. Over the years she has watched over many neighborhood children while parents are out working, struggling to get by on minimum wage. She minds them before and after school and the youngest throughout the day. She prepares lunch for those who come home at noon. She brings them to church on Sundays so that they hear about their heavenly Provider who cares for them as his beloved children. As the years have gone by, many of the children are now adults who still keep in touch, sharing happy events and seeking prayer for life's challenges. One thing for sure they all know is that Eleanor's love hasn't changed whether they are big or small.

Visiting her home recently, I was inspired by her "wall of fame"—photos of her "kids" lining her hallway. I saw her love for each child as she commented on their talents, achievements, and aspirations. As we slowly moved down the hall, I was impressed with the fact that Eleanor has discovered her true self, all in the process of pouring out her love for her children. She models well the gracious spirit of Jesus as she gives herself away on behalf of her little (and now) big ones. She has seen the command of Christ for what it really is—an opportunity for the receiving and passing on of Christ's neverending stream of love.

The Enigma of the Downward Way

Questions for Reflection:

1. In our popular culture we don't hear a lot about the benefits of self-denial. At best, we might read about the power of delayed gratification in a self-help book *How to Become the Real You in Ten Easy Steps!* Nevertheless, Jesus announces, "If any want to become my followers, let them deny themselves and take up their cross and follow me" (Matt 16:24). In light of this command, it is important to consider what Jesus means. Write down in your journal some of your immediate thoughts on what self-denial looks like for you on a daily basis. Share your ideas with a soul friend to see if you can together get a better hold on what it means.

2. In many world religions—for example, Buddhism, Judaism, Confucianism, Sufism—the theme of suffering plays an important part in one's spiritual transformation. We Christians don't talk about suffering as much, but it actually is a central theme in the life of Christ and in his teachings. Obviously, the imagery of "taking up our cross and following Jesus" suggests that there is going to be a significant dose of it in the Christian walk. How do you see the dimension of suffering as it plays out in the Christian experience? What does the picture of carrying a cross say to you as you consider your relationship with Christ?

Part I: Casting the Vision

3. The apostle Paul employs the language of the "true (new) self/false (old) self" in a variety of his writings (Eph 4:22–24; Col 3:9–11). Jesus does not use the same language in our Matthew text, but the journey towards the new self is a core theme for realizing "true life" (Matt 16:25). In your experience, how does the false self exert itself in your everyday world? What steps do you take to resist these drawings and grasp hold of your true self?

4. As we consider the broader theme of the directives of Jesus, what spiritual disciplines assist you in funding your relationship with Christ? Spend some time journaling what your "spiritual praxis" looks like on a weekly basis. Be specific. Intentionality plays a huge factor in carving out time to spend with the Master Teacher.

Part II

Going Deeper

Chapter 5

The Way of the True Self

God is our true friend, who always gives us the counsel and comfort we need. Our danger lies in resisting Him; so it is essential that we acquire the habit of hearkening to His voice, of keeping silence within, and listening so as to lose nothing of what He says to us. We know well enough how to keep outward silence, and to hush our spoken words, but we know little of interior silence. It consists in hushing our idle, restless, wandering imagination, in quieting the promptings of our worldly minds, and in suppressing the crowd of unprofitable thoughts which excite and disturb the soul.

FRANÇOIS DE FENELON

Fenelon's Spiritual Letters, 145

> *Ask, and it will be given to you;*
> *search, and you will find;*
> *knock, and the door will be opened for you.*
> *For everyone who asks receives,*
> *and everyone who searches finds,*
> *and for everyone who knocks, the door will be opened.*
> *Is there anyone among you who, if your child asks for bread, will give a stone?*
> *Or if the child asks for a fish, will give a snake?*
> *If you then, who are evil, know how to give good gifts to your children,*
> *how much more will your Father in heaven give good things to those who ask him!*
> *In everything do to others as you would have them do to you; for this is the law and the prophets.*

Part II: Going Deeper

Enter through the narrow gate;
for the gate is wide and the road is easy that leads to destruction, and there are many
who take it.
For the gate is narrow and the road is hard that leads to life, and there are few who find it. (Matt 7:7–14)

SITTING ON THE ROCKY CRAG of April Point on Quadra Island, BC, I am mesmerized by the inundating waves wafting upon the rugged shoreline. It is as if each oscillation splashing upon the rocks ends with the hallelujah "Feel the Love!" I hear it also in the elongated cry of the eagle perched high upon a cedar, calling out to its lifelong mate circling on the other side of the bay. I sense it as a mama seal patiently shows its young cub how to break open sea urchins in the shallows. It also beats in the mother otter leading its two young ones back and forth between the wharf and the boats devouring the leftovers of the fishermen cleaning their prizes. And it is reflected by parents training their children in the skills of being in and around ocean waters while fishing, kayaking, sailing, and surfing. All is a manifestation of God's great love pouring out upon his creation as parents of every sort interact in loving actions for the benefit of their young. It strikes me as one gigantic blaze of love energizing everything on land, sea, and air, flowing from the primal source of God's eternal fire of affection.

Not everyone perceives our current state of affairs with this sense of integration. For many, fragmentation and disintegration form the dominant hue. Perhaps it circles back to an ontological theme of whether there is a God or not, and if there is, what is God's nature? In the Scriptures God is experienced in the web of life, and one's fundamental calling is to enter into a relational rhythm with the Divine Family. As the Jewish scholar Abraham Heschel argues, an essential question is "What does the three-lettered word G-O-D mean for us?" Heschel asks us to consider, "Is God a mere word to us, a name, a possibility, a hypothesis, or is He a living presence?"[1] Hence, in our own ruminations, is the name of G-O-D merely a hypothetical abstraction, or does G-O-D refer to a blazing fire drawing us into a profound relationship of love?

Heschel's fundamental query is the one that Jesus continually poses during his Galilean ministry. As we further our reflection on the imperatives of Jesus, more questions emerge from this simple enquiry: What is

1. Heschel, *God in Search of Man*, 9.

our relationship with our Creator God? Is he loving or punitive? Does he refuse or welcome us? Do we embrace or flee from God's presence? Jesus presses his listeners to honestly engage the intricacies of the human-divine connection.

The Open Hand of God

The Master continually reminds us that loving compassion is the key descriptor employed by the prophets to reveal God's nature. God is a good God who loves us passionately and who desires that we enter into a dynamic relationship with him. He does not coerce or order us about as subordinates but invites us to journey with him in a dynamic of intimacy, knowledge, and personal presence.

To this end Jesus paints a picture of a God who listens and desires the best for his children. To make this point Jesus uses the three imperatives of "ask," "seek," and "knock" to demonstrate that we can go to God with confidence as we go to him in prayer. In each case Jesus affirms that God hears our requests and responds positively. If we ask, God will graciously give to us. If we seek, we will find. And if we knock, God will open the door (Matt 7:7). Indeed, Jesus is so concerned that we understand this fundamental truth, that he repeats the commands a second time saying, "For everyone who asks receives, and everyone who searches finds, and for everyone who knocks, the door will be opened" (7:8). This presentation of God does not square with the clichéd rendition of God as a miserly old man in the sky who delights to frustrate his children. Rather, he wants us to be in a constant dialogue with him so that our relationship of love grows in trust, confidence, and goodwill over the entire span of our lives.

To elaborate on this call to action, Jesus gives an example of how parents graciously respond to their children's requests: "If your daughter asks for bread do you give her a stone? Or, if your son asks for a fish do you give him a snake?" (7:8–9). These references may seem a bit strange to modern readers, but in the Middle Eastern context, circular loaves of bread could indeed be mistaken for stones from the shores of the Galilean Sea and eel-like fish could indeed resemble sea snakes. Jesus understands that most parents do not willingly disappoint their children and give them things that may harm them. He highlights this truth by acknowledging that even though people are marred by sin they generally treat their children well. If this be so, how much more can God be trusted to provide for the needs of his beloved children? This argument from the lesser to the greater is a rhetorical device that Jesus often employs, reminding his disciples that God is their loving Abba who wishes the best for them. He is not capricious or angry like the Greco-Roman gods, but is a trustworthy Parent who loves, cares, and provides for the needs of all of his daughters and sons.

The key for Jesus is that his disciples have confidence in Abba and go to him with assurance and not in fear. God is not a vengeful tyrant who is watching for his children to slip up. He knows that we are fragile and broken, but he waits for us with open and compassionate arms. The parable from Luke's Gospel of the two brothers is instructive here as both the prodigal and elder sons are loved by their beneficent father. We know that the gracious father of the parable represents Abba who longs to be in relationship with us. If we show up, he shows up. It is this call to faith and trust that Jesus invites us to take. No matter what our circumstances, even as a little child goes to her parents, we are to go to God in confidence, knowing that God desires the best for us in every situation we face.

Whether times are good or bad, up or down, positive or negative, our practice is to be the same. We are to go to Abba and not give in to the world's discouraging and enervating forces. Ultimately, the choice is ours in how we respond to the challenges that life brings. We can play the role of victim and blame God (or others) for life's trials. Or, we can choose the path of Jeremiah, who encourages us to resolutely seek and rest in God: "When you search for me, you will find me; if you seek me with all your heart, I will let you find me, says the Lord, and I will restore your fortunes" (Jer 29:13–14).

Jesus encourages us to take up the practice of daily prayer as a key spiritual discipline for developing confidence in our heavenly Father. Prayer is to be characterized by persistence and stick-to-itiveness as is emphasized through the repetition of the imperatives: First, we "ask," or make our requests known to God. We do this in honest and real terms by revealing what is happening in the corners of our hearts and minds. There are to be no secrets. Everything is laid out before our loving God. It is essential that we maintain this type of open communication with God or our relationship with him becomes stunted.

Second, we "seek" God by resolutely keeping him the center of our lives. Kierkegaard reminds us of this focus in his refrain to "keep willing one thing," which means maintaining Abba as our focal point regardless of circumstances. It is this type of enthusiasm that Paul models for us as he addresses the Galatians, "[that] it is no longer I who live, but it is Christ who lives in me. And the life I now live in the flesh I live by faith in the Son of God, who loved me and gave himself for me" (Gal 2:20). It is a daily seeking and drinking at the well of Jesus that propels us forward in the spiritual life.

Third, Jesus invites us to keep "knocking" on heaven's door so that our relationship of intimacy grows with our heavenly Creator. Day in and day out, like waves on a seashore, we are to keep coming to the door of our loving Abba. As we do so our relationship with him deepens and the incredible riches of Christ lead us into the strong arms of our loving God.

The Way of Love

Jesus ends his discourse with a call to action. "In everything *do* to others as you would have them *do* to you; for this is the law and the prophets" (Matt 7:12). This statement stands as a bookend to the Sermon on the Mount's opening volley which reads, "Do not think that I have come to abolish the law or the prophets; I have come not to abolish but to fulfill" (Matt 5:17). We have come to identify this refrain as the "Golden Rule" as it summarizes both the law and Jesus's radical teaching.

We know that the central tenet of the Golden Rule was also propagated by other teachers. For example, the Athenian orator Isocrates stated, "What you do not want done to yourself, do not do to others," and Rabbi Hillel maintained that he could sum up the entire law while standing on one leg![2] The particular edge of Jesus's teaching is his emphasis that the true motivation for keeping the law is sacrificial love. It is not simply about avoiding maltreatment but the proactive sharing of God's compassionate love. The entire Torah is guided by a love for others rather than a spirit of self-interest where we risk division into opposing factions. When we concentrate on the well-being of our own group and devalue the importance of the stranger, indifferent to his or her legitimate needs, we reveal an irrational fear that there is not enough to go around.

In contrast, the kingdom isn't about taking care of our perceived needs and preoccupation with what we want to receive from others, but a true desire to live out the principles of God's reign. We do this by imagining ourselves to be in the situations that others experience, and then act in a way which is mindful of their well-being. Jesus identifies this sense of

---

2. Mounce, *Matthew*, 66.

awareness as the way of love and argues that it reflects the core values of the law and prophets. Consequently, as Christ's followers, we are invited to embrace the path of compassion, patience, and generosity as we walk with and before others. It is a similar refrain of the prophets who call for "justice roll[ing] down like waters, and righteousness like an ever-flowing stream" (Amos 5:24) and "He has told you, O mortal, what is good; and what does the Lord require of you but to do justice, and to love kindness, and to walk humbly with your God" (Mic 6:8). It is this intentional proclamation of *agape* love that ushers in the kingdom of God.

The link between Jesus's teaching on prayer and his call for compassion is this disposition of love. Love is the foundation between Abba and his children. So it is to be replicated between Jesus's disciples and their neighbors. The New Testament continues to echo this position: "In this is love, not that we loved God but that he loved us and sent his Son to be the atoning sacrifice for our sins" (1 John 4:10); "I give you a new commandment, that you love one another. Just as I have loved you, you also should love one another" (John 13:34); "Love never ends . . . and now faith, hope, and love abide, these three; and the greatest of these is love" (1 Cor 13:8, 13). The Scriptures encourage us repeatedly to live our lives in a manner which depicts God's love. His amity takes precedent over any other cultural, societal, or religious mores. Nothing is to supersede our compassionate concern for others—neither ethnicity, gender, race, nor economic standing.

As we welcome the refugee, immigrant, or newcomer into our midst, treating them with dignity, we imitate our Father in heaven who is Lord of "every family in heaven and earth" (Eph 3:15). In contrast, when we divide ourselves into factions and look down on others in contempt, we act in a manner which diverges from "the way of the righteous" and mirrors the "way of the wicked." The apostle John cautions us about choosing this path of divergence as he writes, "Do not love the world . . . for all that is in the world—the desire of the flesh, the desire of the eyes, the pride in riches—comes not from the Father but from the world. And the world and its desire are passing away, but those who do the will of God live for ever" (1 John 2:15a–17).

The Way of the True Self

Jesus's sermon concludes with four contrasting examples that illustrate his call to action: two types of roads (Matt 7:13–14), two types of fruit (7:15–20),

The Way of the True Self

two types of disciples (7:21–23), and two types of builders (7:24–27). For our immediate purpose, our focus is on the first set of contrasts—the two different paths which humanity chooses to travel.

The first road that Jesus describes is a spacious highway which he characterizes as "wide, easy, and well-traveled," and seemingly the most popular route. This congested freeway stands as a metaphor for the self-centered life in which the false self is dominant and one's ego is front and center. As a person travels this path choices are made through the lens of self-regard, self-advancement, and self-glorification. Such a pathway is controlled by the instinctive needs of childhood as seen in survival, security, affection, self-esteem, power, and control. These desires are not bad and are indeed necessary for one's survival during infancy. The challenge occurs when as adults we make these characteristics the central dynamic of our lives as they truncate our capacity for self-maturation and disinterested compassion.[3] When we travel this road it becomes all about our own desires and any concern for our neighbor is pushed into the distant background. Furthermore, this self-centered lifestyle creates a dislocation in our relationship with God. Such a lifestyle creates a growing indifference to the well-being of others and this is a true sign of walking on the wide and well-traveled way.

The self-centered path contrasts with the narrow, hard, and seldom traveled road, which Jesus says, ends in life rather than loss. It is a trail which is tight and restricted, where one has to persevere and work hard to finish the course. The metaphor of the hard road represents the way of the true self which is governed by love, compassion, and good will towards others. When we travel this path, God is honored and kindness and justice for all take precedence over our personal advantage. In the language of another metaphor, the narrow road suggests that we are taking off the false (old) self and are putting on the true (new) self as the Apostle Paul enjoins, "strip off the old self with its practices . . . and clothe yourselves with the new self, which is being renewed in knowledge according to the image of its creator" (Col 3:8–10). Living in this manner, we align ourselves with Jesus's love and build our lives on his teaching.

Now we are like the individual who builds his house on a sure foundation and not simply on sand because it is easy and offers little resistance. Jesus concludes his lesson by encouraging his listeners to build properly (and I paraphrase): "If you build your house well, it will stand against the flood of life's challenges, but if you construct it poorly it will be overcome by the

---

3. See Keating, *Dios se manifiesta*, 106–7.

vicissitudes of life" (Matt 7:24–27). If we hear and act on the words of Jesus, we become like the person who builds on solid rock and whose journey is characterized by life (7:14). The sage of old paints a similar picture as he summarizes the contrasting ways that people live their lives:

> Happy are those who do not follow the advice of the wicked, or take the path that sinners tread, or sit in the seat of scoffers; but their delight is in the law of the Lord, and on his law they meditate day and night. They [the righteous] are like trees planted by streams of water, which yield their fruit in its season, and their leaves do not wither. In all they do, they prosper. . . . The Lord watches over the way of the righteous but the way of the wicked will perish. (Ps 1:3, 6)

The road that ends with abundant life is characterized as the hard or restricted way—hard or restricted because it is characterized by an unreserved focus for listening to God's word. Rather than bopping around to current popular fads, there is an unfettered commitment to hear the voice and call of Abba.

It is a way of life grounded in the Lord's Prayer where God's kingdom is desired, established, and ameliorated through compassionate love. We travel this narrow and pressed-in path as we "ask, seek and knock" on heaven's door and continue to place ourselves in the hands of the Master. Doing so we understand that we belong to God and that he empowers us for the demanding work of reconciliation. Our conversation with him is not an attempt at manipulation, but it is an honest dialogue in sharing the details of our lives and having confidence that he acts on our behalf amidst life's challenges. Such an approach goes beneath the shallows of our immediate concerns and penetrates the deeper realm of listening and attending to God's presence.

It is this daily rhythm of conversational prayer that enables us to press on and not abandon the hard way for the way of "non-choosers and half-choosers [who] live in the immature condition of wanting to "play everything by ear."[4] The way of "willing one thing" equips us to maintain our equilibrium, make difficult choices, and not be distracted by the constant barrage of competing voices. As we tread this path, we draw Jesus in and out with every breath, and confidently advance on the narrow, but fruitful way.

---

4. Van Breemen, *Let All God's Glory Through*, 23.

The Way of the True Self

Walking the Line

As we have seen, Jesus is not only the way, but he is also the gate (Matt 7:13) by which we pass through to experience abundant life. John the Evangelist speaks to this specific truth as Jesus announces, "I am the gate. Whoever enters by me will be saved, and will come in" (10:9). We enter through the gate as we come into relationship with Jesus, stay on the path, and keep listening to his voice. The power of perseverance comes from the promptings of the Holy Spirit who lives within us, even as Jesus encouraged in Luke's parallel Sermon on the Plain, "How much more will the heavenly Father give the Holy Spirit to those who ask him!" (Luke 11:13).

From our side of the equation it is about making intentional choices to follow and obey the Spirit's leading. The connection between obedience and listening is not accidental, but rooted etymologically: "obey" comes from the root "to listen." When we choose to listen and obey, the Spirit guides us in his ways so that we are not left to our own devices, but are led by the indwelling presence of Jesus.[5]

Listening interiorly to the voice of Jesus becomes the animating influence of our decision making in both time and space. As we quiet our minds in silence, we settle into an assurance of Jesus's compassionate inhabitation which guides us forward in real time. When we engage this practice of listening, it becomes the essential thing to make time to meet with Abba daily so that our hearts and minds are filled with his loving presence. Jesus encourages his disciples to pursue this spiritual discipline: "Whenever you pray, go into your room and shut the door and pray to your Father who is in secret; and your Father who sees in secret will reward you" (Matt 6:6).

Considering Jesus's admonition, we can identify a threefold pattern: (1) establish a personal time with God for the purposes of listening to his voice ("go into your room"); (2) quiet your heart to overcome the distractions of the day ("shut the door"); (3) sit in his presence and experience his healing and refreshing presence ("pray to your Father who is in secret"). A measure of silence and solitude helps us to develop this form of prayer. The goal is to develop a habitual practice of meeting with God so that our interior life is fostered and our capacity for spiritual receptivity remains strong.

It is critical to keep tuning into the Spirit's leading at each point of the day. As we listen in such an attentive way, the Spirit of God keeps us

---

5. See Gal 5:18 and Eph 5:18. Saint Paul uses the names of the Spirit and Jesus Christ interchangeably with the shared meaning of the indwelling presence of Christ. See Bruce, *International Greek Commentary on Galatians*, 144.

grounded and energized for kingdom living. By "walking the line," we travel light, and in the words of Ambrose, we "resemble fish that pass though life's storms rather than snails which are overburdened by the burdens they carry on their backs."[6] If we do the opposite, with our focus on our own inward state, our problems become more daunting and we become more and more anxious! Jesus encourages us to come to him and give him our anxieties and burdens so that his rest rises up in our hearts. Similarly, the psalmist directs us to rest in God's arms: "But I have calmed and quieted my soul, like a weaned child with its mother; my soul is like the weaned child that is with me" (Ps 131:2).

The point is we are to go daily to our Shepherd God and rest in his comforting presence. How we shape the contours of this practice is up to us, but it is essential that we consistently go to him if we are to "walk the line" of Christ. If we draw back and run on our own steam, it is inevitable that we will lose the motivation and energy to stay on the narrow and hard path. As a counseling friend once advised me, the waters of our well must be filled up and we do it by meeting with Abba and allowing his Spirit to fill us. If we don't, the exigencies of life assuredly wear us down, and by default we end up on the wide way, which takes us in the opposite direction of God's *shalom*.

A Final Comparison

Jesus concludes his sermon with a telling contrast of two types of believers (Matt 7:21–23). In it he compares those who claim to know God but do not act commensurately and those who actually hear and obey the teachings of Jesus: "Not everyone who says to me, 'Lord, Lord,' will enter the kingdom of heaven, but only the one who does the will of my Father in heaven." Through this cautionary word Jesus underlines the importance of living authentically before God, not playing self-serving games in false-self mode, and truly engaging the gospel on a daily basis.

Choosing this path doesn't mean that we never make wrong choices for we are full of limitations. Yet, there is a genuine desire to live faithfully amidst the challenges of navigating a complex world. Such determination represents the path of seeking God in our everyday lives and in a fashion that resonates with the fruit of the Spirit. As we "walk the line" we let go of

---

6. Cited in Kidner, *Psalms 73–150* in reference to Ps 84:7, "they go from strength to strength."

things that divide us and separate us from others like "impurity, jealousy, anger, envy, malice, and dissension," and put on the positive attributes of "joy, peace, kindness, generosity, patience, and above all, love" (Gal 5:19-26). By taking off the old clothes of narcissistic behavior and replacing them with the new wardrobe of compassionate love we act in a manner which radiates the values of God's new kingdom.

Now the way of the true self differentiates itself from the false self as we let go of anxiety and freneticism and put on the clothes of peace, tranquillity, and a gentle spirit. The true self understands the specific call of God and stays on point with the few concerns that flow from God's hand. We cannot do everything or take up every fight. If we find ourselves living in such a manner, then we are most likely slipping back into the old ways of self-centered striving and egotistical behavior. No! We are called to receive from our Father in Heaven the selected crosses we are to bear and let others carry their own. Thomas Kelly is helpful here: "We cannot die on *every* cross, nor are we expected to."[7] Entering the narrow gate that leads to life does not mean saving the world but addressing the true concerns that God has laid on our hearts for the benefit of others and for the work of his kingdom. At times we immerse ourselves in a church subculture because we have a difficult time saying "No." We don't want to disappoint others or fear falling off the religious radar of being known, appreciated, and esteemed. Or we go in the opposite direction and refuse to embrace any cross at all! It is important to remember that the way of following Jesus is indeed demanding and hard, but it is also the enlivening way that leads to abundance and true life.

---

7. Kelly, *Testament of Devotion*, 83.

Part II: Going Deeper

Questions for reflection:

1. When you say the word G-O-D, what does this three-letter word mean for you? Does G-O-D refer to a mental concept or a living presence? How does this work itself out in your daily routine?

2. As we have seen, the Scriptures often compare two ways of living—one which is self-focused and the other God-centered. The following passages speak to aspects concerning these two ways of life. Take time to pray over these passages and then journal your thoughts on how they apply to your present faith journey:

    "Seeing that you have stripped off the old self with its practices and have clothed yourselves with the new self, which is being renewed in knowledge according to the image of its creator." (Col 3:9–10)

    "As God's chosen ones, holy and beloved, clothe yourselves with compassion, kindness, humility, meekness, and patience." (Col 3:12)

    "Above all, clothe yourselves with love, which binds everything together in perfect harmony. And let the peace of Christ rule in your hearts, to which indeed you were called in the one body." (Col 3:14–15).

3. Jesus invites us to go to Abba with an attitude of "asking," "searching," and "knocking." How do you express this dynamic of seeking God as you interact with your friends or colleagues at work? Spend some time journaling about how you converse with God in the everyday of your life.

4. The way of Jesus is described as a hard way, but it is not a frenetic way (Matt 11:30). If you are feeling overcome by a hectic schedule you may find that its root lies in your own desire to please others or you have difficulty in saying "no." What steps might help you in getting control of your schedule? Think through your use of time and effort to reevaluate what might be the best use of your time and spiritual gifts.

Chapter 6

An Anchored Faith

> Christian faith occurs in the *encounter* of the believer with him in whom he believes. It consists in communion, not in identification, with him.... Faith is a history, new every morning.
>
> KARL BARTH
>
> *Evangelical Theology*, 99, 103

> *In the morning, when he returned to the city, he was hungry. And seeing a fig tree by the side of the road, he went to it and found nothing at all on it but leaves. Then he said to it, "May no fruit come from you again!" And the fig tree withered at once. When the disciples saw it, they were amazed, saying, "How did the fig tree wither at once?" Jesus answered them, "Truly I tell you, if you have faith and do not doubt, not only will you do what has been done to the fig tree, but even if you say to this mountain, 'Be lifted up and thrown into the sea,' it will be done. Whatever you ask for in prayer with faith, you will receive." (Matt 21:18–22)*

THE JOURNEY OF FAITH can never be reduced to a series of rules or regulations that we religiously follow. Neither is faith simply an intellectual exercise that we read and sign as a contract or mortgage application. Such a reductionist approach is doomed to fail since it won't energize us for the demanding challenges that life brings our way. Instead, we need a dynamic relationship of love with our God whom we obey, worship, and daily experience. It is a faith which Karl Barth aptly sums up as an "encounter ... new every morning."[1] Only an intimate ongoing exchange between the Divine Family and ourselves will enable us to overcome the pressure from the world that challenge the logic, values, and propositions we hold dearly.

For such reasons Saint Paul encourages us with the aspirations of "life in the Spirit," "Christ in me," "living by faith," and "living by the Spirit"—interchangeable phrases reminding us that faith is not simply a lifeless idea or theory. It is a dynamic, living relationship with our triune God revealed as Father (Parent), Son, and Spirit.[2] The resurrected Christ lives in us through his Spirit. It is this powerful indwelling that motivates and empowers us to move forward in the journey of faith. If it were simply up to us to provide the energy for our spiritual pilgrimage, we would fail and become deeply embittered in our failings. For this reason, the spiritual writer Henri Nouwen avows that it is by faith that the follower of Christ remains positive and does not take up the role as victim.[3] The apostle John exclaims that we are not overcome by the forces of evil but are indeed "overcomers" through the power of Christ's enabling Spirit who dwells within us (1 John 5:4–5, NIV).

To this end, it is essential that we listen to Jesus's voice as it pertains to faith and the central role it plays in our spiritual lives. As we overhear Jesus in intimate conversation with his band of disciples, we also receive his direction for future ages, including our own cynical and skeptical culture. Let's keep listening to Jesus's imperatives and see what rises up in our own hearts as we are attentive to his voice.

A Fruitless Fig Tree

These are heady times for Jesus. Entering Jerusalem on a donkey, he has fulfilled the ancient prophecy which foresaw the Messiah's victorious entrance into the holy city (Zech 9:9). He has cleansed the temple of its crude commercialism by overturning the tables of the money changers and demanding that the temple return to its place as a house of prayer and worship (Matt 21:12–13). Of course, in doing so, Jesus has piqued the anger of the religious establishment who benefited from the economic practices related to the temple. Exhausted from a grueling day, Jesus leaves the city and travels to the nearby village of Bethany where he and his disciples spend the night with friends for needed rest. Up early the next morning, Jesus

---

1. Barth, *Evangelical Theology*, 103.
2. See Bruce, *International Greek Commentary on Galatians*, 144.
3. Roderick and Nouwen, *Beloved*, 37.

returns to the city with his band of companions to resume his ministry of sharing God's word. On the way he sees a fig tree by the side of the road. It is early in the season, but from past experience he anticipates finding some figs to satisfy his and his entourage's hunger. He is surprised when not a single one is to be found.[4] Disappointed, but always a master teacher, Jesus turns his letdown into a valuable teaching opportunity: "May no fruit ever come from you again!" Before their eyes the tree immediately withers (Matt 21:19). Now over the past three years the disciples have seen many miracles, but this one truly amazes them. They burst out in unison, "Wow! How did that just happen!"

To make sense of this puzzling scene, we need to back up a bit and understand the greater context of the nation's and specifically the religious establishment's resistance to Jesus's ministry. By and large, they do not receive his message of good news and reject his role in the loving overtures of Father God. Instead, the ancient oracles of the prophets ring true which speak of the nation's resistance to Yahweh as seen through the symbol of the unfruitful fig tree: "When I wanted to gather them, says the Lord, there are no figs on the fig tree; even the leaves are withered, and what I gave them has passed away from them" (Jer 8:13); "Ephraim is stricken, their root is dried up, they shall bear no fruit " (Hos 9:16); "Woe is me! For I have become like one who, after the summer fruit has been gathered, after the vintage has been gleaned, finds no cluster to eat; there is no first-ripe fig for which I hunger" (Mic 7:1).

Instead of receiving the message of God's generous love, the majority of the populace reject Jesus's instruction and prefer the nominal, legalistic religion of the day. They have no interest in producing spiritual fruit but prefer the status quo of mediocrity, personal comfort, and the charade of empty peace. To this end, the people and leadership of Israel resemble the barren fig tree as they demonstrate complacent and hardened hearts. Pausing before the fruitless tree Jesus underlines the truth that there is a need for receptive hands and responsive hearts to experience the blessing of God.

Fruitful or Fruitless Spirituality

Israel is not alone in possessing a recalcitrant spirit. In our hearts we know that at times we also resist the movement of God's Spirit. Instead of seeking

---

4. The commentator Mounce observes that the smaller figs of the first harvest were usually available at Passover time. *Matthew*, 197.

his will, we seek our own will; and instead of working for his kingdom, we strive for our own kingdom. Alas, where there should be fruitfulness there is barrenness due to our reticent and self-serving hearts. This is not only a personal challenge. It is also a stumbling block for the community of faith. The church, too, dwindles and dies when it withdraws from the Spirit of God.

It is imperative that the collective body of Christ remains rooted in the power and presence of Jesus if it is to stay healthy and bear spiritual fruit. Jesus underlines this very point in another context when he shares with his disciples, "Abide in me as I abide in you. Just as the branch cannot bear fruit by itself unless it abides in the vine, neither can you unless you abide in me. I am the vine, you are the branches. Those who abide in me and I in them bear much fruit, because apart from me you can do nothing" (John 15:4–5). Connected to Christ, the church is a dynamic power. Apart from him, it diminishes and perishes for he is its true soul food. Even as cut flowers appear beautiful for a short while, so the church loses its beauty and ebbs away when it is disconnected from Jesus. Our collective power and spiritual energy are linked to the Lord of the church. Apart from him "we do nothing." In ourselves we do not have the capacity to bear spiritual fruit. This truth is particularly germane for the contemporary community of faith as we blithely trust in statistics, socioeconomic data, and demographic studies. Many churches have waned for reasons other than changing demographics and socioeconomic shifts. It is essential that we stay rooted in Jesus or we quickly resemble the fruitless fig tree.

The same truth is illustrated in the broader context with the story of the rich young ruler who approaches Jesus on the road to Jerusalem (Matt 19:16–20). The story speaks of a pleasant young man coming to Jesus and asking, "What good deed must I do to have eternal life?" In response, Jesus refers him to the law and the keeping of the commandments to which the man replies, "I have kept all these; what do I still lack?" The sincerity of the youth greatly impresses Jesus, as suggested by Mark's account that "Jesus looked at him and loved him" (Mark 10:21). To clarify his intention and probe the youth's response, Jesus adds a significant detail, "Okay, one more thing: Sell all you have and give the proceeds to the poor, and come and join my band." At this point, the drachma drops for the young man as he realizes the ramifications of following Jesus, and he sadly turns and walks away, because as Matthew observes, "he had many possessions."

The import of the narrative for the modern reader should not be lost as we hear Jesus's telling conclusion, "Truly I tell you, it will be hard for a rich person to enter the kingdom of heaven" (Matt 19:23). This narrative serves as a spiritual paradigm for our wealthy, consumer-based society which esteems possessions, money, convenience, technological gadgets, and individual comfort. Like the rich young ruler, we also are attracted to the wisdom, noble values, and compassionate service manifested in the life of Jesus, but frequently we draw back due to our attachments to wealth, pleasure, and personal ease. We turn away (sadly?) because we are not willing to give up our stuff and status for Christ, who seeks the well-being of all people and not just a few. As such, we resemble the barren fig tree which offers no nourishment for Jesus and his hungry band of disciples.

Faith's Essential Role

The disciple's amazement regarding the withering of the fig tree evokes a startling affirmation from Jesus. He invites his disciples to pursue a dynamic relationship with their heavenly Father radiating assurance and confidence in his loving compassion. To emphasize this point he frames his exhortation with the couplet "have faith and do not doubt" (21:21), which does not reference a special kind of faith, as much as a true faith, even if it is "the size of a mustard seed" (Matt 17:20). Jesus's call for a living faith includes what Erik Erikson addresses when he speaks of "trust rather than mistrust" and its importance for healthy psychological development.[5] Similarly, a true faith is established upon a basis of trust, an essential quality for producing a life of fruitful living. Jesus reinforces his call for a vigorous faith through the use of hyperbole saying that "even if you say to this mountain—perhaps Mount Olivet itself—'Be lifted up and thrown into the sea,'" it will happen because of the robustness of your trust. The vignette concludes with Jesus's summation of prayer's effectiveness: "Whatever you ask for in prayer with faith, you will receive" (21:22).

To appreciate the significance of Jesus's words, we must understand them as they relate to his concern for God's kingdom and the roles we play in this greater narrative. It is not about seeking what is best for ourselves but about how God's story unfolds through our lives and actions. Clearly Jesus does not present God as a genie in a bottle who responds to our requests on demand. Nor does Jesus suggest that our enemies will miraculously

5. McLeod, "Erik Erikson's Stages of Psychosocial Development," 8.

disappear as we send out a heavenly S.O.S.! Rather, his concern is for us to be active agents in God's story as we live out our everyday.

We catch a glimpse of the interplay between faith and God's glory in an earlier story from Matthew's Gospel. The account centers on Jesus coming to the aid of his disciples who are caught up in a powerful storm while at sea (Matt 14:22–33). In the narrative, Jesus walks upon the water toward the fearful disciples, speaking words of peace as he approaches their little boat. Peter's response to Christ is particularly telling here: "Lord, if it is you, command me to come to you on the water." Peter steps out in faith onto the water and takes a few bold and successful steps. The Gospel writer tells us that soon Peter becomes distracted by the strong winds and rolling waves and in fear begins to sink. Jesus takes his hand, and brings him safely to the vessel. And then Jesus muses to the disciples, "You of little faith, why did you doubt?" I am not sure how a soaking wet Peter receives such an admonishment, but the story certainly illustrates the astounding power that Jesus wields and the impact upon believing hearts.

God calls us, as well, to a relationship of intimacy—of faith, not doubt—through the spiritual discipline of conversational prayer. We are invited to meet with him as our "Abba! Father!" who is able to do incredible things through us as we act in faith and partner with him for the purposes of his kingdom.[6] As ordinary Christians we can overcome seemingly impossible circumstances through trusting in God's power and relying on his compassionate presence. Hence, as Jesus addressed his disciples about faith and its power to move mountains it is fitting for us to entertain analogous questions: What spiritual mountains exist in our lives that we want Abba Father to move? Are there spiritual hurdles that continue to trip us up where we need Abba's overcoming empowerment? The good news is that Jesus dwells within us. As we abide in him, his strong spirit loosens the enemy's hold and frees us to serve him in new and fruitful ways. It is not about garnering personal accolades or gaining notoriety but serving the High King with passion, enthusiasm, and a faithful heart.

As we continue to "walk the line" we learn that we often meet Jesus in surprising places and in situations we would not consider ideal. We do not have the luxury of determining the most appealing path forward or calling all the shots on our spiritual journey. God always remains the prime actor in our human-divine story and the way to fecundity is to have receptive

---

6. See Gal 4:6; Rom 8:15; Mark 14:36.

hearts heeding the Spirit's leading and unstopped ears hearing his gentle whispers.

What is unproductive on our parts is to be double-minded so that we roll about on the waves of life's challenges and take our eyes off the one who anchors our souls.[7] Such vacillating minds whirling about in the past or the future do not have the capacity to act decisively. In this state we are not able to comply with Jesus's imperative from the Sermon on the Mount to "let your word be 'Yes, Yes' or 'No, No'; anything more than this comes from the evil one" (Matt 5:37). Living our lives by faith means that we are listening to God's voice, "new every morning," and remain attentive to it as we proceed throughout our everyday.[8]

The old adage holds true that if we cannot be choosers we become "non-choosers and half-choosers" which keeps us stuck and unresponsive to the Spirit's leading.[9] When we walk through life's maze, following the crowd and refusing to make the hard decisions which free us to follow our God-given vocations, we shortchange ourselves. Seeing into our timid hearts, Jesus calls for bold and courageous action which enables us to say "yes" to the Spirit's enlivening and creative presence. As Rolheiser proposes,

> While that presence is never over-powering, it has within it a gentle, unremitting imperative, a compulsion toward something higher, which invites us to draw upon it. And, if we do draw upon it, it gushes up in us in an infinite stream that instructs us, nurtures us, and fills us with endless energy.[10]

Such intimation is not aggressive, but it is clear.

Fruitful Discipleship

Jesus's commentary becomes foundational counsel for future generations of believers. We are called to live confidently before God knowing that he travels with us in every situation. The assurance of his indwelling presence is a needed counterweight to the fatalistic ennui of our modern culture. The predictably negative news reports create an overriding sense that hopeful change is impossible and any sense of optimism is fleeting. Bound by this

---

7. See Jas 1:6–7.
8. See Barth, *Evangelical Theology*, 103.
9. See Van Breemen, *Let All God's Glory Through*, 24.
10. Rolheiser, *Wrestling with God*, 104.

cynical mindset, it is easy for us to slip into a victim role and a belief that we are powerless to meet life's challenges. In contrast, recognizing these enervating proclivities, Jesus enjoins us to trust in God's reassuring presence which funds us in overcoming life's obstacles. Hopelessness may be the mood of the day but the Spirit of God empowers us to make positive choices and to live creatively for his kingdom. Indeed, our triune God liberates us from the snares of a gloomy and despairing worldview and enables us to press forward as stewards of God's grace with hope and passion within a needy world.

A crucial outcome of Jesus's ministry is that he gives us the capacity to live lives characterized by abundance rather than scarcity. The firstfruits of God's kingdom communicate that there is more than enough to meet the world's needs rather than a fundamental insufficiency that our society bemoans. The feeding miracles of Christ emphasize this very point that God's kingdom is shaped by plenitude rather than sparsity.[11] Erik Erikson is once again instructive as he observes that healthy human development includes a dynamic of "generativity rather than stagnation." In level seven of his eight stages of psychosocial development generativity is referred to as "making your mark on the world through creating or nurturing things that will outlast an individual."[12] The authentic human experience is characterized by fruitfulness rather than a submission to the world's devitalizing forces emanating from "isms" of every shade and stripe. In spite of seemingly daunting actualities, we are called to live with gratitude and enthusiasm as we pour our energy into matters that alleviate the human condition. As a result, we are able to make a real difference to the lot of individuals and communities as we go forward in the name of Jesus.

Over the years I have seen such an impact on countless youth through the ministries of our local community center. Recently a young couple walked into our Sunday worship service. As I greeted them, I recognized the young man as a former youth who had been nurtured through his time at Frontlines. Indeed, the couple had recently been married at our church by our family pastor who happened to be the director at the center during those formative years. Pastor Bonnie had such an influence on his life that he wanted her to marry them a dozen years later. During our conversation I learned that Jason is now a teacher and has a passion for helping other youth navigate life's challenges. As the service began and we concluded our

---

11. See Matt 15:32–39; Mark 8:1–9.
12. McLeod, "Erik Erikson's Stages of Psychosocial Development," 8.

chat, I was reminded again that the spirit of love continues to advance as it flows from one individual to another. For some, it heals, consoles, and inspires; for others it encourages, motivates, and mentors. For all of us, love touches us deeply, softening our hearts, and evokes a receptivity to the divine caress.

A Dynamic Combination

As Jesus has emphasized in his encounter with the fruitless fig tree, our faith is funded by an active and regular prayer life. When we live our day in a prayerful spirit we can enjoy the assurance that "Whatever we [you] ask for in prayer with faith we [you] will receive." Such an approach to our everyday strengthens us amidst the vicissitudes of life that we regularly face. Indeed, as two leading theologians insist, prayer acts as a rejuvenating force which opposes the banality and apathy that characterizes our culture.[13] A scuba diver inflates a BCD to counterbalance the heavy weights necessary for submersion. Likewise, prayer lifts us up, counteracting the heavy burden of our culture's perspective.

Through prayer we are able to maintain a fresh and vibrant relationship with Jesus because we know interiorly that his Spirit is with us in every situation. As the writer of Hebrews enjoins, "He never leaves us or forsakes us" (13:5–6). This truth enables us to persevere in hope even as we experience his grace—aptly called "the smile" of God. To this end, even as a ship engages stabilizers to reduce its roll due to wind and waves, prayer acts as a dynamic stabilizer. Life's trials keep rolling in, but trust and confidence in God stabilize us so that our ship of faith is not shipwrecked.

Prayer is critical as it strikes at the heart of our desire to control the exigencies of life. We have an inveterate need to manage things and to orchestrate every part of our day. The mantra of Western culture (and often of our churches, as well) is "to be strategic." As we adopt this slogan, we blithely board the utility train singing, "efficiency, efficiency, efficiency. (As an aside, this tendency was viewed by Thomas Merton as the most pressing monastic problem of his day!)[14] Prayer, on the other hand, embraces the truth that spiritual fruitfulness cannot be equated with statistics, money, or management charts, but is engendered by faith in the abundance of God.

---

13. Rahner and Metz, *Courage to Pray*, 27.
14. Rolheiser, *Holy Longing*, 32.

Part II: Going Deeper

Rather than desperately trying to fix (and organize) things, we need to wait on the Spirit's movements which in time reveal *kairos* opportunities and paths of blessing. The words of Isaiah remind us not to rush ahead and trust in our own insights: "For my thoughts are not your thoughts, nor are your ways my ways, says the Lord. For as the heavens are higher than the earth, so are my ways higher than your ways and my thoughts than your thoughts" (55:8–9). The instructive way forward is to cultivate an attentive heart which waits upon the Divine Voice, give up our obsession for control, and open our hearts to the sweet stirrings of the Spirit.[15]

The combination of faith and prayer enables us to accomplish great things for God's kingdom as we rely on the power of his indwelling Holy Spirit. As we listen for his voice through a variety of spiritual disciplines including silence, solitude, meditation, and spiritual reading or *lectio divina*, and continue to feed on Jesus as our soul food, we will be amazed at the accomplishments of the Spirit in and through us.[16] In his diminutive book *Beams of Prayer*, Edward Farrell reminds us that faith plays an essential role in our ability to "walk the line," and I close this chapter with his insightful observation:

> The disciple is the one who is close enough to hear and to respond to Jesus's deepest question, "Do you believe me?" (John 11:26). Everything depends upon my answer! My faith, my ministry, my lifestyle, my prayer, is anchored in my faith in Him as present with me, "always going before me" (Matthew 28:7).[17]

Together, as the bride of Christ, we are empowered to engage in life-changing actions that transform our neighborhoods for the glory of God.

---

15. See also Pss 5:3; 27:14; 33:20; 37:7, 34 for references of "waiting on God."

16. See helpful works on spiritual reading including Foster, *Celebration of Discipline*; Willard, *Divine Conspiracy*; Davey and Davey, *Abba's Whisper*.

17. Farrell, *Beams of Prayer*, 88.

Questions for Reflection:

1. Karl Barth describes our walk with God as "a history new every morning." By this he means that our ongoing encounter with God is to be dynamic and alive. It is not a mere routine or something that speaks to a past event. In your journey with God, how do you nurture your spiritual relationship so that it is indeed "new every morning"?

2. As you have reflected upon the curious story of the fruitless fig tree what has come up for you in your meditation? Have there been any new insights? In what ways does it resonate with your journey at this point in time?

3. In your journal write down your thoughts on what spiritual fruitfulness looks like as you consider your relationship with Abba. Jot down five ways that you think you are bearing spiritual fruit. It might be in terms of relationships at home or at work, or service that you offer at church or in your community. Name the specific fruit(s) you are producing and spend time praying over these areas of fruitfulness.

PART II: GOING DEEPER

4. Jesus connects the reality of bearing fruit and an active prayer life. Take a few moments to reflect upon your prayer practice and how it interfaces with your areas of fruitfulness. Are there ways you might strengthen this connection to support your spiritual output?

5. Erik Erikson addresses the two areas of "trust rather than mistrust" and "generativity rather than stagnation." In your journal spend some time writing about the connections between these two levels of development. What possibilities open up as you imagine links between these stages of growth? Share your thoughts with a close friend and see what bubbles up in your discussions.

Chapter 7

The Dangers of Judgmentalism

The glorious liberty of the children of God is not the happy fluttering of a butterfly from one attractive flower to another. It is joyous, but it is also radical, hard, and absolute . . . Giving us our burden, God launches us into an unsuspected adventure, a conflict, which is finally that of freedom.

JACQUES ELLUL

The Ethics of Freedom, 124–25

> *Do not judge, so that you may not be judged. For with the judgement you make you will be judged, and the measure you give will be the measure you get. Why do you see the speck in your neighbor's eye, but do not notice the log in your own eye? Or how can you say to your neighbor, "Let me take the speck out of your eye," while the log is in your own eye? You hypocrite, first take the log out of your own eye, and then you will see clearly to take the speck out of your neighbor's eye. (Matt 7:1–5)*

IN HIS BOOK *Tattoos on the Heart*, Gregory Boyle shares powerful stories of his relationships with gang members as a priest in the city of Los Angeles. Looking back over his sojourn he recognizes that for a number of years he was trying to save young people through his own efforts, and because of it, came close to burning out. Eventually he learned that the only way to reach them was through love—showing it over and over. To that end he sums up his experience:

> There is no force in the world better able to alter anything from its course than love. Ruskin's comment that you can get someone to remove his coat more surely with a warm, gentle sun than with a cold, blistering wind is particularly apt. Meeting the world with a loving heart will determine what we find there. We mistakenly place our trust too often in the righteousness of our wind, though we rarely get evidence that this ever transforms anything . . . sooner or later, we all discover that kindness is the only strength there is.[1]

Boyle's observation "that kindness is the only strength there is" connects us with Jesus's encouragement to love one another and his strong rebuke for casting judgment upon others. I think we experience a certain tension on hearing Christ's command not to judge recorded in Matthew's Gospel. It's a tough one to figure out. It seems contrary to much of what we have been taught and what our culture deems important—the need for critical thinking, evaluating opposing viewpoints, and the necessity of competing for rank and position. Consequently, this particular command is puzzling, and we need to work hard to hear Jesus's words afresh.

A Curious Command

The exhortation of Jesus is clear and emphatic: "Do not judge one another," in which he repeats the word "judge" (*krima*) four times to make his point in two short verses (Matt 7:1–2)! Since the actual word Jesus uses means "stop criticizing one another," it seems there is a great deal of irritation and acrimony going on amidst his followers. I can imagine that Jesus didn't enjoy being surrounded by negative and critical folk any more than we do today. In the early days of building an effective team such negativity would be especially damaging. To ward off any rancorous sentiment, Jesus addresses his disciples directly, ordering them to refrain from all censorious judgments. A caveat, of course, remains in that Jesus does not say that it is impossible to discern error in another person's behavior. Indeed, such discernment is demonstrated as Jesus expands his argument in advising individuals to be wise in sowing the seed of faith (Matt 7:6) and to be able to identify false prophets who show up and create confusion in the congregation (7:15–20). There is a place for such acumen in maintaining a healthy

---

1. Boyle, *Tattoos on the Heart*, 124.

and vibrant community, but a harsh and critical spirit only creates a spirit of distrust, enmity, and severed relationships.

Jesus develops his point by employing a popular Jewish adage: "you will receive as you give out" (7:2). The idea sounds a little like a belief in *karma*. But this is not quite what Jesus is suggesting. He is encouraging his listeners to adopt a reciprocal principle between giving and receiving. "Give, and it will be given to you. A good measure, pressed down, shaken together, running over, will be put into your lap; for the measure you give will be the measure you get back," he says in another place (Luke 6:38). Lifelong conversion is the name of the game, requiring a need for self-examination before correcting anyone else. Jesus acknowledges a similar sense of correlation in the Lord's Prayer reminding us that our debts are forgiven as we forgive the debts of others (Matt 6:12). Hence, it is imperative that we look at ourselves and our own behavior before we evaluate and examine the actions of others.

And the underlining truth is that we are *all* to be involved in the process of transformation. It is not simply about changing the other person! If there is to be any vitality and joy within the broader community, it is necessary for all to be on the path of renewal, not just a few. Destructive criticism is counterproductive. When we put others down or seek to expose their faults, it simply doesn't create a happy and peaceful environment. Rather, it establishes a foreboding atmosphere that keeps people on their guard. A critical and judgmental attitude shuts people down, causing them to circle their ranks and hide their true thoughts and feelings. Such interaction is sad and becomes a barrier for living creative and fruitful lives for the glory of God.

An experience on a dive boat made this phenomenon quite real for me recently. We were diving the aqua blue waters of Little Cayman on a famous site notoriously named Bloody Bay Wall. Due to its challenging but appealing reputation, there were a string of boats anchored along the wall—a busy dive site. After an exhilarating experience with abundant fish and coral life, we completed the dive and climbed back aboard. As we were getting out of our gear we saw a new diver sitting on the deck, and before we could say "hi," she started into her story of how she mistakenly got on our boat, breaking an unspoken rule to make sure you get on your own craft—a challenging feat under these sea conditions. She announced in penance that "she was walking the walk of shame"! At this point I couldn't help myself, and blurted out, "Hey, there is no shame here. We all have done something like this somewhere along the line"! I wanted her to know that we were not judging her, and if anything, were amazed that she had traveled so far, seeing her boat in the distance. Eventually a small zodiac came and collected her and she left us with smiles and a big wave. As she departed, a line from Van Breemen flashed through my mind and it felt like a heavenly hug, "Every person needs more love than he or she deserves."[2] In my mind my thoughts rang out, "Yes, that's me too!" The truth is that usually the best thing is to simply shut up and not say the unnecessary and unhelpful words that just make people feel bad. They already feel bad enough.

The Carpenter's Workshop

As a carpenter Jesus knew a lot about the cutting of wood and stone. Watching his father working in the shop, he had learned the pertinent skills to become an effective tradesman. He was familiar with the variations of woods—oak, juniper, sycamore, and eucalyptus—and their specific characteristics comprising colors, weights, and applications. He had probably experienced the irritation of having a speck of sawdust lodged in his eye and knew its impact upon clear sight and movement around the workshop. As a result, in verse three, when Jesus contrasts the differences of a "beam" (*dokos*) of wood used in the building of a large structure such as the temple and a "speck" (*karphos*) of debris caught in one's eye, he understands from experience what he is talking about. It is plainly a bit of Eastern hyperbole illustrating well the difficulty of making accurate judgments in stressful times. An individual simply cannot assess a situation correctly when such encumbrances impede one's vision.

Jesus reinforces his point by employing a parallel line in the form of a question, "How can you say to your neighbor [or, brother, as the NIV indicates], 'Let me take the speck out of your eye,' while the log is in your own eye?" (Matt 7:4). The implication is that it is impossible to make a clear judgment under such duress. Rather, a process of self-evaluation and honest personal reflection needs to take place before venturing into the realm of criticizing others. As Jesus observes elsewhere, kindness and mercy are to be the foundation for our relationships, rather than our own righteousness, as we ourselves are desperately in need of God's mercy. All of us are broken vessels, so let us be compassionate with each other rather than zealous to judge the faults of our brothers and sisters.

2. Van Breemen, *God Who Won't Let Go*, 21.

Jesus highlights the importance of this truth in the parable of the two debtors (Matt 18:23–35). As the parable reads, one of the individuals is forgiven a massive debt of ten thousand talents (worth fifteen years of a laborer's wages) but fails to forgive a friend with a much smaller debt (about four months' wages). This failure results in the second person being thrown into prison. When the landowner hears of this ironic turn of events he confronts the ungrateful tenant saying, "Why were you not kind with your neighbor even as I was sympathetic with you? Don't you recognize the inconsistency in your behavior by not forgiving his paltry sum when I had forgiven your massive debt?" Fitly, the tables are turned once again, and the unforgiving tenant is thrown into prison and suffers the pains of his own ingratitude.

When we engage in criticism we erode relationships of trust. This is especially evident with petty fault-finding, which Jesus highlights when referencing an irritant (*karphos*) lodged in one's eye. Such behavior engenders a sense of discouragement and separation between people. When we travel this road, relational decline is inevitable, distance grows, and relationships begin to fall apart. The book of James emphasizes this destructive pattern: "How great a forest is set ablaze by a small fire! And the tongue is a fire. The tongue is placed among our members as a world of iniquity; it stains the whole body, sets on fire the cycle of nature, and is itself set on fire by hell" (3:5b–6). These are strong words, but they spell out what we all know to be true when we ourselves experience critique, judgment, and shame. And it is magnified when the faultfinder is incapable of seeing their own faults and acts as if he or she is free from the very actions criticized. This type of self-deception heightens the irony found in Jesus's illustration when a person critiques the minor infractions of others while blatantly committing high crimes.

The Failure of Hypocrisy

Jesus concludes his exhortation about judging others with a strong censure: "You hypocrite, first take the log out of your own eye, and then you will see clearly to take the speck out of your neighbor's eye" (Matt 7:5). Borrowing the term "hypocrisy" from the theater world, meaning "play a part," Jesus underlines the fact that we are not playing a role in a drama production, but are living our lives in the real world where people are impacted for good or bad by our words and attitudes.[3]

To accurately assess the actions of our neighbor, we must feel the weight of our own brokenness and engage in a rigorous practice of self-examination. In candid personal reflection we must not gloss over our personal shortcomings but identify and name them before proffering any measure of critique. Apart from this self-awareness, we are bound to misconstrue the actions of others. Furthermore, by using the word "to see clearly" (*diablepo*), which literally means "to open one's eyes wide," Matthew reinforces the necessity of having true "in-sight" prior to any process of examination. We must first see ourselves unequivocally if we have any hope of discerning the nuances and behavior of others.

There must be an operation of self-confrontation before there can be a tête-a-tête with others. We share the same human condition; the identical passions which manifest themselves in others swirl around in our own hearts and minds. Because of this affinity, there is a need to honestly consider our own spiritual walk if we are to authentically engage someone else concerning the ups and downs of their spiritual meanderings. As the authors of *Compassion* make clear, "The evil that needs to be confronted and fought has an accomplice in the human heart, including our own."[4] As a result, it is critical that we are a part of the transformation activity, which includes clear evidence of self-reflection, otherwise we misjudge the actions of others due to the blinders that we personally don.

The poignant film *The Green Mile* highlights this truth as it tells the story of John Coffey who is wrongfully convicted of raping and killing two young white girls in Louisiana and awaits his end on death row, known as "the green mile." The judgment against him is based upon his ethnicity as an African American, his imposing physical stature, and his proximity to the bodies when they are found. Unknown to the judge and jurors is Coffey's extraordinary empathic ability which allows him to vicariously experience the pain of others. When the police locate the girls' bodies, they find Coffey uncontrollably sobbing while holding them, not for a crime he had committed, but out of empathy for their tragic end to life. The reality of the situation is completely lost on everyone except a prison guard named Paul Edgecomb who comes to understand Coffey's story, his heightened

---

3. "Hypocrisy" is a favorite word of Matthew who uses it 13 of the 17 times employed in the New Testament. See Mounce, 54.

4. McNeill, *Compassion*, 125.

The Dangers of Judgmentalism

spiritual gift, and the truth that he is innocent. Edgecomb attempts to intervene judicially for Coffey but is unable to convince the authorities, and ironically is the one designated to execute him for the murders he didn't commit. The film addresses the significant hurdles individuals face in making accurate and proper evaluations as a beautiful, gentle man is convicted of a fabricated crime based on racism, prejudice, and superficial analysis. As a result, he is judged hastily and incorrectly, due to the preconceptions of others who are driven by their own biases, fears, and miscalculations.

The takeaway here is that it is difficult for us to be truly objective in our criticism of others. Impartiality is a challenge as our own baggage gets in the way. We often jump on the faults and practices of others while secretly pursuing (or wishing to pursue) the same behavior. Our sight is unclear and we improperly assign blame where it is not deserved. Jesus makes this point in the parable which includes a Pharisee who fasts and tithes for everyone to see while in his heart condemning a tax collector who stands nearby praying. Yet, as Jesus concludes, God sees the Pharisee's proud heart and the publican's repentant one as he prays, "God, be merciful to me, a sinner!" In application, Jesus highlights the truth that the tax collector "went down to his home justified rather than the other [the Pharisee]; for all who exalt themselves will be humbled, but all who humble themselves will be exalted" (Luke 18:14).

It logically follows that it is wise to be slow in making an appraisal of others, for we normally do not see the entire situation and easily miss the mark while drawing our conclusions. Again, the letter of James offers helpful commentary: "If any think they are religious, and do not bridle their tongues but deceive their hearts, their religion is worthless" (1:26). Better to practice the way of the mystic John of the Cross, positively impacting every situation while focusing on encouragement, "Where there is no love, put love and you will find love."[5]

---

5. It is worth noting that this statement is an excerpt from a letter in response to a prioress concerned for his welfare, not part of the formal writings of John of the Cross. It has attracted a number of authors such as Dorothy Day, cofounder of the Catholic Worker movement, with slight variations in the translations. John of the Cross, *Collected Works of St. John of the Cross*, 760.

Part II: Going Deeper

Turning from Judgmentalism to Compassion

As the church of Christ, it is vital to work together in a spirit of trust and mutual respect. Since we toil with each other as a group of volunteers, everyone is encouraged to take up the virtues of patience, humility, and compassion so that the community of faith is not easily fractured. Each day we must remember our common goal of laboring is for the cause of Christ so that we are not divided by our partisan interests. Rather than a penchant for legalistic practices which eclipses our central commitment to love, forgiveness and mercy must be at the core of all of our actions.

Pursuing amity means that we do not create a double standard by judging others while excusing ourselves for the same actions. Hypocrisy of this sort is a subtle process which reveals itself slowly over time. It is not as if we declare ourselves to be hypocrites for all to see. Rather we slip and then slide down its convoluted path and end up as the proverbial king who wears no clothes. We need to wake up and honestly examine ourselves so that we see others clearly and remain true to our foundational calling of love.

The movement towards hypocrisy is fed by an inveterate commitment to dualism. We tend to pigeonhole others into predetermined categories of black or white, right or wrong, good or bad, gay or straight, Protestant or Catholic. We travel this road because we feel uncomfortable with ambiguity and want to declare a specific position to be certain and true. Our complex global world with its massive diversity and variation does not lend itself to drawing with such straight lines. Dualistic decision-making regularly misses the mark and lamentably reinforces the differences between people groups. We may long for clear-cut polarities such as "my correct understanding" and "your incorrect one," but the complexities of life derail our narrow and simplistic perspectives. Richard Rohr cautions us on adopting such an easy but misguided frame of mind: "Binary thinking is not wrong or bad in itself . . . but it is completely inadequate for the major questions and dilemmas of life." Indeed, as he underlines, there are times when it is important to make "either/or" judgments to survive our crazy world, but that is not an excuse for being judgmental of other people's actions and beliefs.[6]

---

6. Rohr, *Naked Now*, 32.

The Dangers of Judgmentalism

Going Forward in Tranquility

What helps us to move beyond judgmentalism? I suggest two disciplines of the heart that lead us in this direction: living with awareness and living with gratitude. The significance of awareness is evident in both the Gospels and the Epistles, as illustrated in Jesus's request for his disciples to "watch with him" as he prays in Gethsemane (Mark 14:34), and in Paul's exhortation to the Corinthians to "keep alert, and stand firm in your faith" (1 Cor 16:13).

The imperatives to "keep watch" and "stay alert" are invitations to live in the present as opposed to our predilection of rolling around in the past or the future. If we fixate on the past we often find ourselves mired in shame or guilt for prior actions and if we live in the future we find ourselves caught up in the anxieties of future unknowns. The Scriptures encourage us to give up such fearful proclivities and live in the present moment which is shaped by the love of God. The apostle John speaks to this reality when he writes, "There is no fear in love, but perfect love casts out fear" (1 John 4:18). The call is to stay in the arms of Abba who deeply loves us and will never let us go regardless of past failures or future challenges. Let us drill down deep into the substratum of God's limitless love, and from the security of this safe place, experience his caring, constant, and consoling presence.

When we remain in the present moment God reassures us that he is with us. Here. Now. Regardless of challenges that may emerge down the line. Thomas Merton refers to this place of quiet and stillness as the "point vierge"—a place of rest, where we find succor in God's loving arms of goodness, peace, and tranquility.[7] In this place of presence there is no need for judging others as we leave all of our worries and queries to the One who discerns all. The writer of Hebrews enjoins, "And before him no creature is hidden, but all are naked and laid bare to the eyes of the one to whom we must render an account" (Heb 4:13). As a result, we can be still and rest in Abba's love while repeating our "yes" to the Spirit who works in us and is never foiled in achieving his purposes.

A second tool for constraining a judgmental disposition is to practice the spiritual discipline of gratitude. The apostle Paul highlights this truth throughout his writings: "Give thanks to the Father, who has enabled you to share in the inheritance of the saints in the light" (Col 1:12); "Devote yourselves to prayer, keeping alert in it with thanksgiving" (Col 4:2); "Give

---

7. Merton, *Conjectures of a Guilty Bystander*, 131–32. See Callahan, *Spiritual Guides for Today*, 100, 112, on *le point vierge*.

thanks in all circumstances; for this is the will of God in Christ Jesus for you" (1 Thess 5:18); "Do not worry about anything, but in everything by prayer and supplication with thanksgiving let your requests be made known to God" (Phil 4:6). Such an intentional practice of giving thanks enables us to rest in the confidence that God ultimately makes all things well.

We do not need to become anxious over life's annoying disturbances. We do not need to take on the role of "gatekeeper" to protect God's kingdom from the invading hordes. Our job is to be available for God's work, to be responsive to his daily leading, and to enjoy his gifts with thanksgiving. Thomas Kelly emphasizes the value of such a serene trust: "We need not get frantic. God is at the helm. And when our little day is done we lie down quietly in peace, for all is well."[8] Such an approach fosters a spirit of humility and frees us from censorious attitudes as we imitate our servant God who is loving and compassionate towards all of his creation.

Resting in "the point *vierge*" does not mean that everything that happens in any given week is going to be positive. We know from experience that this is simply not the case. Indeed, as someone in my congregation said to me, "In any given week ten things will happen of which seven are good and three are bad." This is the truth. We need to accept it and not be surprised by it. Life is not all of one piece. It wasn't for Jesus and it won't be for us either. Life is indeed a mélange of good and hard times. It is the same for everyone. The challenge we face is that we usually dwell on the three bad things and forget the seven good that happened in the same week. We also forget the truth that God is able to bring good even out of our hard times.

Life is full of obstacles but God is greater than them all and even in our trials we are able to find rest in his consoling arms. The key is to keep looking to God in faith so that our suffering does not become useless but fruitful. This fecundity happens as we allow Abba to work in us even during our times of suffering so that in all seasons of our spiritual journey our spiritual maturation process continues. Perhaps it is for this reason that Jesus observes that our Father in heaven prunes his vines so that the maximum quantity of spiritual fruit comes to harvest (John 15:1–5). God works in our lives in good times and bad. Nothing is lost. Let's keep looking to him through open eyes of faith even as he empowers us to do our part for the exquisite tapestry that the Spirit is weaving in God's new creation.

---

8. Kelly, *Testament of Devotion*, 100.

The Dangers of Judgmentalism

Questions for Reflection:

1. Judging others just seems to be a way of life. Everyone does it. So when we hear Jesus speak so strongly about not judging we are taken back. Spend some time journaling about Jesus's statement, "Do not judge so that you may not be judged" (Matt 7:1). What are some first steps you can take to try to follow this instruction?

2. Jesus encourages us to engage in a serious process of self-evaluation before offering any critique of others. What might be an example in your own life of taking a speck out of someone else's eye while a log exists in your own eye?

3. Hypocrisy is a word from the theater culture, referencing an actor who is playing the part of a character in a play. In real life pretending to be someone that you are not is deceitful. As you consider your own faith journey can you identify areas where you play the role of a hypocrite? How does this make you feel and what might you do to change your behavior?

4. Rather than judging others we are called to be compassionate with one another. Have you seen examples where compassion is more fruitful than judgmentalism? Why do you think this is the case? Jot down in your journal what it looks like.

Part II: Going Deeper

5. We have reflected upon the two spiritual disciplines of "practicing awareness" and "practicing gratitude" to help overcome judgmental attitudes. Spend some time journaling about these spiritual disciplines and how you might incorporate them in your day-to-day walk.

Chapter 8

Love Is Something That You Do

> It is when we stand in the righteous all-seeing light of love that we can dare to look at, admit, and *consciously* suffer under this something in us which wills disaster, misfortune, defeat to everything outside the sphere of our narrowest self-interest. So a living relation to God is the necessary precondition for the self-knowledge which enables us to follow a straight path, and so be victorious over ourselves, forgiven by ourselves.
>
> Dag Hammarskjöld
Markings, 2.24.57,149

> *You have heard that it was said, "You shall love your neighbor and hate your enemy."*
>
> *But I say to you, Love your enemies and pray for those who persecute you, so that you may be children of your Father in heaven; for he makes his sun rise on the evil and on the good, and sends rain on the righteous and on the unrighteous. For if you love those who love you, what reward do you have? Do not even the tax-collectors do the same? And if you greet only your brothers and sisters, what more are you doing than others? Do not even the Gentiles do the same?*
>
> *Be perfect, therefore, as your heavenly Father is perfect. (Matt 5:43–48)*

JESUS'S COMMAND TO LOVE one's enemies startles, and even offends us, when we think about what it means to love. Love connotes ideas of strong affection for or attraction to another person—what C. S. Lewis explains as

"Need-loves" in his work *The Four Loves*. He explains, "We are born helpless. As soon as we are fully conscious we discover loneliness. We need others physically, emotionally, intellectually."[1] He identifies four different strands of love, of which the first three derive primarily from need. The first is *storge*, or affection, which is a demonstration of familial love and funds the power of families and relationships of kinship. *Philia* addresses the love between friends, sometimes in abundance and sometimes hardly at all. A third contour of love is *eros* speaking to the dynamic of sexual passion which we call "being in love," and can be the source for creative energy in every sphere of existence. All these expressions of love are active in the functioning of our day-to-day world. We know that everything goes better when these loves are practiced and are globally present.

Yet there is a fourth love which the Scriptures laud and Lewis notes, as a distinct "Gift-love"—*agape* being its Greek name. *Agape* is a giving of oneself for the benefit of others. *Agape* exhibits a disinterested love, moving beyond the limitations of self-interest to actively pursuing the well-being of the "other." And it is *agape* which Jesus addresses as he commands us to love our neighbor and our enemy in the Sermon on the Mount. As essential as the first three loves are in the story of humankind, it is *agape* which maximizes our capacity for turning the world upside down, becoming the foundation for something we do and not simply feel.

Not Feelings but Actions

The Sermon on the Mount begins with an imaginative structure as Jesus references an Old Testament law and then clarifies its meaning by interpreting it in new and fresh ways. He does this on six occasions using an oppositional formula which reads as "You have heard that it was said . . . but I say to you."[2] It is the last of these pairs which concentrates on our focus of *agape* love: "You have heard that it was said, 'You shall love your neighbor and hate your enemy.' But I say to you, 'Love your enemies and pray for those who persecute you'" (Matt 5:43). The most likely Old Testament passage available for Jesus's comparison is found in Leviticus: "You shall not take vengeance or bear a grudge against any of your people, but you shall love your neighbor as yourself: I am the Lord" (19:18). Interestingly we note that it doesn't include a corollary statement calling for the "hating

---

1. Lewis, *Four Loves*, 7.
2. See the six occasions in Matt 5:21, 27, 31, 33, 38, 43.

of one's enemies." Nevertheless, in an ancient Near Eastern culture committed to the custom of reciprocity, there is no doubt that its practice was commonplace.

Jesus tells his disciples to replace hate with *agape* love, manifesting an honest concern for their well-being instead of pursuing any form of retribution. As such, Jesus's instruction represents a radical reversal: hate is replaced by love, debasement by kindness, and oppression by mercy. What is particularly striking in Jesus's groundbreaking approach is that love is to be demonstrated by an active intercession for one's enemies. Instead of calling down vengeance, one is to lift them up before the Father in prayer. Such an imperative is psychologically instructive as Jesus knows that praying for one's enemies demands an inner orientation of repose rather than one of agitation.

As we step back and observe such intercession, it makes sense on a number of fronts. First, it maximizes the health of the entire community when personal animosity is replaced with kindness, as illustrated in the Scriptures by caring for an enemy's wayward animals (Exod 23:4–5), or providing the necessities of life for an enemy in need (Prov 25:21–22). Second, it is better not to seek vengeance on an enemy, for God may choose to do the same to you (Prov 24:17–18; Job 31:29). Third, from a leadership perspective, it is more effective to practice mercy than to dole out punishment, as a gentle hand is more persuasive than one that is heavy. Collectively, these points suggest that the broader community benefits when love rather than hatred is the motivation for action. Furthermore, when prayer replaces judgment, all kinds of blessings are made possible as the cycle of reciprocity is replaced with the power of enlivening love.

A telling example of compassion overcoming hatred is found in the film *Three Billboards Outside Ebbing, Missouri*. The story focuses on the tandem of Mildred who has lost her daughter in a brutal rape and murder and the local Police Chief Bill Willoughby who investigates the case with little success in breaking it. Mildred forces Willoughby's hand by contracting a series of billboards to highlight her daughter's murder and embarrass the chief for his seemingly tardy efforts. At the same time, it is revealed that the chief is suffering from cancer and is struggling with its effects during the investigative process.

It is at this juncture that the plot makes a hard turn and illustrates our point at hand. Chief Willoughby's sidekick Officer Jason Dixon, who struggles with anger, prejudice, and alcoholism, is enraged by the news that his beloved captain is gravely ill. In frustration he lashes out against his perceived enemies. He initiates his carnage by attacking businessman Red Welby, who had initially rented out the billboards to Mildred, sending him to the hospital by throwing him out a second-story window. Later, through an unlikely series of events, Officer Dixon ends up sharing the same hospital room with Welby due to injuries from a bar brawl. Both men are covered in bandages so initially they don't recognize each other. But soon enough the truth comes to light.

The grace-filled moment takes place as Dixon, who is confined to bed, reaches for a glass of water but is unable to reach it. At first, Welby shows no interest in helping his unsolicited roommate. However, from somewhere deep in his consciousness, grace bubbles up and he makes his way over to Dixon's bed and hands him his cup of water. Gratefully, Dixon receives the cup, sips the water, and with tears in his eyes, thanks his one-time enemy for his demonstration of kindness. In this brief exchange a secret is unlocked. You and I are able to move beyond the law of reciprocity. An "eye for eye" mentality can be replaced by benevolent forgiveness and it happens through the intentional giving and receiving of compassionate love.

A Family Likeness

We are called to love our enemies because we are called to emulate our Father in heaven. Jesus identifies us as "children of your Father in heaven" which is certainly an elevated status and resonates with the apostle Paul's invitation "to be[come] imitators of God, as [his] beloved children" (Eph 5:1–2). Two examples are given by our Master Teacher illustrating God's provision for every person in every nation and within every culture. The first is that God makes his sun rise on "the evil and the good"; the warmth of the sun shines on everyone and every place. Second, God provides rain "on the righteous and on the unrighteous"; every people group, regardless of moral behavior or faith tradition, experiences the fulsome blessings that spring forth from the celestial vaults (Matt 5:45).

Jesus's words reinforce the expansive nature of the Old Testament Scriptures: "The Lord is good to all, and his compassion is over all that he has made," writes the psalmist (145:9). God's word to Jonah is a case in point: "And should I not be concerned about Ninevah, that great city, in which there are more than a hundred and twenty thousand people who do not know their right hand from their left, and also many animals?" (Jonah

4:11). The same spirit is manifested in Paul's message to the inhabitants of Lystra, "He has not left himself without a witness in doing good—giving you rains from heaven and fruitful seasons, and filling you with food and your hearts with joy" (Acts 14:17). As Nolland in his commentary on Matthew reminds us, a "creational kindness" is established in the Scriptures which expresses God's beneficence to the totality of humankind, and it is this operational kindness that the children of God are to mirror in everyday living.[3]

Jesus emphasizes God's inclusive goodness and his expectation for the disciples to do the same by pointing out that there is no particular virtue in showing affection within the confines of one's own group. While it is a good thing, it is not worthy of acclaim, for even a despised group such as the "tax-collectors" do the same (Matt 5:46). Furthermore, if we shake hands and hug only those in our own circle, we are no better than "the Gentiles" who treat their own friends and family in a similar manner (5:47). The core idea here isn't to demean the tax collectors and Gentiles but to illustrate the truth that our enemies equally express kindness within their own sphere. Therefore, we can conclude, Jesus is pushing us toward a higher standard of loving both neighbor and enemy.

The teaching of Jesus in this portion of the Sermon on the Mount is as critical today as in the Greco-Roman age. The political rhetoric of our own day is highly polarized. People see things in an "either/or" framework: "I am right, you are wrong," "I am good, you are bad," "I am liberal, you are conservative," "I am a capitalist, you are a communist." Such reductionist thinking simply leads to hatred, bigotry, prejudice, and ultimately, violence. An alternative perspective is essential for our survival: We must embrace an altruistic perspective which sees across boundary lines and refuses to be hedged in by issues of ethnicity, creed, language, or nationalistic fervor.

Jesus provides us with such a viewpoint in the parable of the Good Samaritan which he shares in response to a question concerning the identity of one's "neighbor." We know the familiar details: It is the story of a man beaten and left for dead on the road between Jerusalem and Jericho. In the aftermath of the attack, a priest who travels the road sees the wounded man and skirts by on the other side. A little while later another religious individual (a Levite) comes along and similarly walks around the dying person. It is noted that both of the individuals share the same ethnicity as the injured man. Surprisingly, a third person comes along, a Samaritan,

3. Nolland, *Gospel of Matthew*, 268.

who stops and dresses his wounds, and even brings him to an inn where he pays for his ongoing recovery. As he concludes the parable Jesus asks the lawyer the salient question, "Who do you think acted as a neighbor to the afflicted man?" Without pausing, the lawyer answers, "The one who showed him mercy," to which Jesus enjoins, "Go and do likewise" (Luke 10:29–37). The point Jesus is making is that we are to surpass the world's approach by expressing compassion to those beyond our special interest groups. People tend to show cordiality to those who comprise the same identity and kinship. What is needed is a greater vision where all are accepted and deemed to be worthy of kindness, love, and respect. Not only one's friends but also those who fall into the categories of outsiders are to be treated with grace and fairness. It is this groundbreaking teaching from Jesus which turns the world upside down as we incorporate it into our everyday practice. Brother Carlo Carretto summarizes the impact of this truth:

> When Jesus tells me, "Love your enemy," he indicates the maximum possibility and capacity for loving; and at the same time he offers me the maximum hope of having peace on earth. By besieging my enemy with love and not with weapons, I facilitate in him and in myself the possibility of seeing that day dawn when "calf and lion-cub will feed together and a child will put his hand into the viper's lair, and none will harm the other."[4]

Peace flows when we walk in peace. Kindness flows when we emulate the Good Samaritan. Compassion flows when we follow God's rich counsel. To this end let us not be selective in our expression of mercy but imitate Christ's resplendent character by pouring out disinterested love for all.

The Imperative to Be Perfect

Strikingly, Jesus ends his admonition by calling his listeners to "Be perfect as your heavenly Father is perfect" (Matt 5:48). Hearing these words may cause us to become deflated, perhaps musing, "Well that leaves me out! I am nowhere near perfect! I may as well give it up right now!" It is highly unlikely that this was the intention of Jesus's charge. What might be the implication for us as contemporary readers? We note that the word "be perfect" in the Greek text is *teleios* which can be translated as "be complete, become integrated, be mature." It is an uncommon verb in the New

---

4. Carretto, *Essential Writings*, 101.

Testament only employed on three occasions. Here Jesus's command "to be perfect" concludes the six antitheses found in the opening strophes of the Sermon on the Mount and acts as a concluding summons for the entire unit. As such, it represents a call to action for prospective disciples, which could be paraphrased, "As potential disciples, you have heard the elevated status of your calling. Will you now take up the challenge, make your declaration, and come and follow me?"

Jesus's command is an entreaty for wholeheartedness in living out the good news, and may well be based upon the Deuteronomic statute, "You must remain completely loyal to the Lord your God" (Deut 18:13). The underlining truth in it all is to keep pressing forward in our pursuit of God. We are called to take up the kingdom mandate and as Kierkegaard says, "keep willing one thing," for there is no room for holding back or looking over our shoulder at the things we have left behind.

Matthew makes the same point when he tells the story of Jesus and the rich young ruler. In this exchange a youthful admirer comes to Jesus asking what he has to do to become one of his disciples. Jesus's answer is direct, "You need to keep the commandments." The potential follower affirms with an equal degree of paucity that he has done so since his adolescence and presses Jesus to shed more light on his spiritual quest. Jesus pushes ahead with a more demanding step, "If you wish to be perfect, go, sell your possessions, and give the money to the poor, and you will have treasure in heaven; then come, follow me" (Matt 19:21). Hearing the stringency of this new demand, the young ruler slowly turns away, as he doesn't want to give up his great wealth.

Looking more closely we notice that Jesus employs the descriptor "be perfect" (*teleios*) as a way to address the nature of his interlocutor's desires. He peers into his heart and recognizes the vice-like grip affluence has on his life and that he will never venture forward interiorly until he deals with his attachment to the good life. For him to be free he must let go of his prosperity and even his false understanding of himself. Then he will know the liberation of following Jesus and proceed on the path of spiritual maturation. In *Mere Christianity*, C. S. Lewis uses colorful language to describe the implications of Jesus's imperative:

> The command *Be ye perfect* is not idealistic gas. Nor is it a command to do the impossible. He is going to make us into creatures that can obey that command. He said [in the Bible] that we were "gods" and He is going to make good His words. If we let Him—for

> we can prevent Him, if we choose—He will make the feeblest and filthiest of us into a god or goddess, a dazzling, radiant, immortal creature, pulsating all through with such energy and joy and wisdom and love as we cannot now imagine, a bright stainless mirror which reflects back to God perfectly (though, of course, on a smaller scale) His own boundless power and delight and goodness. The process will be long and in parts very painful, but that is what we are in for. Nothing less. He meant what He said.[5]

As we reflect on the rich young ruler's proclivities it becomes evident that "perfection" is demonstrated in a lifelong conversion process—in Lewis's words, at times perhaps very painful—whereby we continually give our lives over to the Holy Spirit's direction. It is not a one-time event. It is true (in most cases) that at a specific time in our life journey, we made a profession of faith—our "fundamental option," as Bernard Lonergan names it—in Jesus's name. However, it is also true that this original choice needs to be reinforced by an ongoing "yes" to the work of the Spirit in our lives. It is this continuous movement of conversion (or sanctification) that leads us into authenticity and "perfection" as commanded by Jesus.

Furthermore, the imperative to be "perfect" is also an injunction to be compassionate, part of the "greater righteousness" that Jesus espouses at the beginning of the Sermon on the Mount (Matt 5:20). The Gospel of Luke reinforces this sense of "perfection" in its parallel Sermon on the Plain, "Be merciful, just as your Father is merciful," or as the Jerusalem Bible renders, "Be compassionate, as your Father is compassionate" (Luke 6:36). Again, the apostle Paul writes, we are to become "imitators of God" (Eph 5:1–2). We are to give ourselves over fully to him, throughout all of life's stages, and use the resources he has given us for the betterment of others.

A cogent example is the life of President Jimmy Carter. Following a stunning defeat in the 1980 election, he spent a great deal of time reflecting on what he might do with his post-presidential opportunities. He tells the story of waking up one night suddenly from sleep and blurting out to his wife Rosalynn that he wanted to establish a center for peace in his beloved state of Georgia. Using the resources accrued as a former president of the United States, President Carter and Rosalynn carried on to create the Carter Center in Atlanta, which is an institute for reconciliation and peace studies, addressing issues like housing, medicine, human rights, and education.

---

5. Lewis, *Mere Christianity*, 205–6.

In an interview with Kate Brower, Rosalynn Carter talks about how blessed she and her husband have been to address debilitating diseases like malaria, trachoma, and lymphatic filariasis and help eradicate other afflictions like Guinea worm.[6] She also shares about their work in housing initiatives like Habitat for Humanity which has constructed thousands of homes around the world providing lodging for those in need. To his credit, President Carter remains active in a hands-on way in the building of houses, even into his mid-nineties, and by this continues to be a powerful model of selfless service.[7] Most likely we do not have the connections and resources of Jimmy and Rosalynn Carter, but we can replicate their passion and energy for doing good—"being perfect"—by living in a manner which demonstrates kindness for all, regardless of ethnicity, religious persuasion, or political alignment.

A No-Matter-What Love

Such a calling to compassion and "perfection" means that we don't simply divide our world into two camps—one consisting of friends and the other of enemies. A reductionist approach of this sort inevitably leads to a hatred of one's enemies, undermining Christ's entreaty for *agape* love. Rather than rejecting our enemies, we are called to receive them, even to the degree of praying on their behalf. Jesus is looking for a "no-matter-what" love which supersedes simplistic bifurcations based on nationality, ethnicity, gender, cast, or socioeconomic differences.

A recent failure on a macro level in this regard took place in Bolivia (a country dear to my heart) when the government of President Evo Morales was overturned due to election fraud and was replaced with an interim administration. As a result of this sudden change, the nation was divided into two factions—one supporting Morales and the other the newly formed opposition. The demarcation of the electorate was not unexpected, but the ensuing violence and loss of life was unforeseen as former neighbors were recast as enemies. Such a simplistic worldview that overtly names people as friends or enemies is doomed to fail and is surely incapable of ushering in the inclusive love which characterizes the kingdom of God.

---

6. Brower describes the disease of Guinea worm as, "a debilitating disease that in 1986 afflicted an estimated 3.5 million people a year in Asia and Africa . . . and due to the work of the Carter Center there were only 28 cases in 2018."

7. See Brower, "Simple Way."

Part II: Going Deeper

A "no-matter-what" love is particularly à propos for the new society of the *laos* of God. The church, as the people of God, is to be the vanguard of inclusive love on planet Earth. Wherever the church is found, in whatever corner of the world, followers of Jesus are to be a people committed to *agape* love, transcending tribal, ethnic, nationalistic, or cultural variances. The Christian way is to be a way of love. We are not to dismiss Jesus's command to love our enemies as an unreasonable or impossible charge. It isn't simply a slogan for "doing our best" or "giving it our all." It is a directive which urges us to transcend the world's pattern of reciprocity inevitably promoting a cycle of aggression. Jesus bids us to embrace a higher calling—a vocation of love. Martin Luther King Jr. understood this commitment when he described *agape* love as "the most durable power in the world. This creative force, so beautifully exemplified in the life of our Christ, is the most potent instrument available in humanity's quest for peace and security."[8]

If this is the case, then we are not to brood over our hurts by fanning the flames of resentment and bitterness from past wounds or injuries. We are called to let it go. As debris on the surface of a river floats downstream, so we are to let the negativity drift away, even as we anchor ourselves in God's infinite and indescribable love. Jesus gives us an imperative to be kind and we must acknowledge that we can't demand a better world if we don't begin by changing our own heart.

The command to love our enemies is an invitation to take seriously the mores of God's kingdom and to do so by pursuing a lifestyle shaped by the virtues of kindness, forgiveness, patience, and charity. It is an admonition to make radical choices for love regardless of the circumstances we face in our everyday world. Such a path requires the practice of stripping off the old self characterized by "anger, wrath, slander and abusive language" and to put on the new self, defined by the virtues of "compassion, kindness, humility, meekness, and patience" (Col 3:8–10). In reality, this new mode of being is realized through an ongoing reassessment and recalibration of habitual patterns carried over from the false self. Instead of falling back into our old behavior patterns, we are urged to replace them with a new schematic governed by love. Rather than simply reacting to external stimuli, we are invited to be intentional. Pause. Reflect. Choose. Act. All flowing from *agape* love. A movement such as this does not commonly take place in a once-for-all operation, but reflects a series of steps which redress the shape of our ongoing journey. As aeronautical navigators remind us, a journey

---

8. King, *Words of Martin Luther King Jr.*, 65.

Love Is Something That You Do

from the earth to the moon doesn't consist of a flight path consisting of "straight up and a sharp turn left," but a continuous series of tiny flight alterations which guide the spacecraft to the lunar surface. Similarly, love is best demonstrated in a series of kind and gentle actions which are not mere rejoinders, but chosen steps manifesting God's love for his creation. Acting in such a manner foregoes the fiery backlash, and alternatively selects a considered response which imitates God's expression located in love.

Questions for Reflection:

1. Loving our enemies seems to be an impossible thing to do. We know this because we don't do it very well. A first step in moving forward might be to name your enemies. They can be individuals who treat you badly or even parts of yourself that hinder your spiritual development. Spend some time journaling about the enemies you face in an ongoing way. Be specific and name them. Pray over what you have written and ask the Holy Spirit for guidance to help you address these concerns.

2. God's compassion is showered upon all of creation. He doesn't divide us into winners and losers. Are there ways that you can reach out to folk who are beyond your immediate circle to demonstrate the compassion of God? Perhaps this effort can include individuals you often

Part II: Going Deeper

find annoying and difficult to be around. In the coming week reach out to someone in this category and see what differences it makes.

3. As we have seen, conversion is a process and not a one-time event. With this in mind, how can we grow in the realm of loving folk who are different from us? How can we overcome the fears that have been instilled into our hearts and minds from our youth? Most likely we can't do this on our own, so join with a friend or two to discuss and pray over the barriers that hinder your demonstration of love.

4. Praying for our enemies is a true sign that we are making progress on hearing Christ's commandment to love our enemies. In your quiet time this week include time praying over the enemies you identified in question one.

5. To be perfect seems to be a daunting requirement. If we translate it along the lines of being compassionate or merciful, how does it strike you? How and where can you be more compassionate/merciful in your everyday experience? Think of specific ways and act upon them in the coming week.

Part III

Moving to Maturity

Chapter 9

Authentic Discipleship

We shall not be saved by anything less than commitment and the commitment will not be effective unless it finds expression in a committed fellowship. If we have any knowledge of human nature, we begin by rejecting the arrogance of self-sufficiency. Committed women and men need the fellowship not because they are strong, but because they are—and know they are—fundamentally sinful and weak.

ELTON TRUEBLOOD

The Company of the Committed, 22–23

"Beware of false prophets, who come to you in sheep's clothing but inwardly are ravenous wolves. You will know them by their fruits. Are grapes gathered from thorns, or figs from thistles? In the same way, every good tree bears good fruit, but the bad tree bears bad fruit. A good tree cannot bear bad fruit, nor can a bad tree bear good fruit. Every tree that does not bear good fruit is cut down and thrown into the fire. Thus you will know them by their fruits.

"Not everyone who says to me, 'Lord, Lord,' will enter the kingdom of heaven, but only one who does the will of my Father in heaven. On that day many will say to me, 'Lord, Lord, did we not prophesy in your name, and cast out demons in your name, and do many deeds of power in your name?' Then I will declare to them, 'I never knew you; go away from me, you evildoers.'

"Everyone then who hears these words of mine and acts on them will be like a wise man who built his house on rock. The rain fell, the floods came, and the winds blew and beat on that house, but

> *it did not fall, because it had been founded on rock. And everyone who hears these words of mine and does not act on them will be like a foolish man who built his house on sand. The rain fell, and the floods came, and the winds blew and beat against that house, and it fell—and great was its fall!"*
>
> *Now when Jesus had finished saying these things, the crowds were astonished at his teaching, for he taught them as one having authority, and not as their scribes. (Matt 7:15-29)*

Both the Sermon on the Mount (Matthew 5–7) and the Sermon on the Plain (Luke 6:17–49) conclude with a parable contrasting one who builds a house on sand with another who builds on solid rock. The parable's emphasis is that during a great storm, the house erected on sand washes away while the one constructed on solid rock weathers the storm. The parable contrasts the individual who hears Jesus's words but doesn't act on them with the person who both hears and acts upon God's word. In sum, Jesus's call is for an authentic life—a demonstration of faith in a person who takes his teachings seriously rather than feigned lip service while pursuing one's own interests.

As the unit closes, Matthew adds the telling postscript "that the crowds were astonished at his teaching." Jesus's audience was impressed with his skill, passion, and insightful wisdom. Being impressed, however, is not the same as embracing his teaching. Not everyone follows through and acts upon his instruction. Instead, they resume their day-to-day activities and the pursuit of their own goals. They remain "hearers of the word" but never take it to the next level of becoming "doers of the word." It is one thing to recognize Jesus as a great teacher and model for living a meaningful life, but it is quite another to know him as Lord and be devoted to him in both word and deed.

An earlier story from Israel's time in Persia resonates with the enthusiasm for God's kingdom that Jesus is promulgating. We find it in Esther's words to Mordecai in her aspiration to save the people of Israel: "I will go to the king, though it is against the law; and if I perish, I perish" (Esth 4:16). If we paraphrase Esther's intention it might read as "I will give all I have, even to the point of death, for the sake of God's people." Whether we are in stormy or still seas, Jesus is looking for this type of unfettered passion.

Authenticity or Inauthenticity

Jesus underlines the importance of authenticity by noting that individuals may come prophesying and acting in his name but who are not purveyors of true faith. This comment would surely have piqued the people's curiosity. They understood Malachi to be the last great prophet from four hundred years ago. Now John the Baptist's prophetic ministry has created a great stir with crowds responding to his clarion call to "prepare the way of the Lord, make his paths straight" (Matt 3:3). The Baptist's lifestyle and dynamic delivery of God's word have emphasized repentance and readying one's heart for the Messiah's imminent coming. Since John's death at the hand of Herod, there have been now a host of individuals engaging in prophetic speech. Some Jesus has affirmed and others he has decried.[1] It is this latter group that Jesus signals out, "Beware of false prophets, who come to you in sheep's clothing but inwardly are ravenous wolves. You will know them by their fruits" (Matt 7:15–16). These specious emissaries appear genuine but their conduct does not back up the message they deliver.

The Master Teacher illustrates his concern with an appeal to a tree and its fruit: a healthy tree bears good fruit while an unhealthy one bears bad fruit. Using the tool of reiteration Jesus reformulates his observation to reinforce the pivotal point: a healthy spiritual life engenders positive outcomes, while an unhealthy life begets malfeasance. It is likely that Jesus echoes the words of Ezekiel here when he cautions Israel about the false prophets who offer peace when there is none to be had (Ezek 13:16).

It is worth noting that an early church document called "The Didache" ("The Teaching"), dating about 90 AD, continues to reference the role itinerant prophets played in the community of faith and the method of discerning the good from the bad—namely, that the true prophet does not stay longer than three days or ask for money![2] The salient point for both the early church and for us now is if there is a gap between the message and the lifestyle of the individual, then the church must be on guard and practice a high level of discernment in weighing the prophet's message. Jesus notes that not everyone who claims to know him actually does. Enthusiastic words are not sufficient to verify a true relationship with the Messiah. Rather, Jesus is seeking an honest heart which reveals itself in a life of obedience played out in day-to-day living. Interestingly, he acknowledges

---

1. See Mark 9:35–41.
2. Bettenson, *Documents of the Christian Church*, 65.

that spurious individuals may indeed perform impressive deeds of power (including the casting out of demons) but not have a true connection with him. This truth is indicated by his parting words, "I never knew you; go away from me, you evildoers" (Matt 7:23). The verb "knew you" connotes relationship and not simply an intellectual knowledge or informational awareness.

Jesus looks for a real relationship with someone which happens through an authentic bond between teacher and student. Then an interior awakening occurs, leading us forward on the path of spiritual transformation. We say a firm "no" to pseudo-discipleship and a dynamic "yes" to becoming an authentic disciple of Christ. This spiritual reconstruction process is fostered as we open ourselves to the Spirit of Jesus and give ourselves wholly to his leading. It is a journey of intimacy as the Spirit of Christ moves within us and we know the reality that our Father in heaven is our Abba. The critical point is that we share in "doing" the will of the Father and not merely hearing his words.

Too often we are consumed by surface issues—greed, power, success, or recognition—and we become distracted by the demands of daily life. Hence, we neglect our fundamental calling to be a priest in the work of God's kingdom (1 Pet 2:9). Even the charismatic enthusiasm, of shouting out "Lord, Lord," does not replace the demands of authentic discipleship! What is necessary is a responsive heart ready to say "yes" to the Spirit's leading which flows from the throne room of our triune God.

A Solid Foundation

Jesus turns to a good story to draw his teaching to a close, reaching back to the well-known genres of Israel's literature to incorporate images that his audience is familiar with. He contrasts the wise and foolish individuals as seen in the wisdom books: "The wise of heart will heed commandments, but a babbling fool will come to ruin" (Prov 10:8) and "The heart of the wise inclines to the right, but the heart of a fool to the left" (Eccl 10:2). He speaks of the prophetic voice portraying the hearer of God's word as one who has listened to a pleasant tune and then immediately goes off and forgets it. As Ezekiel rues, "To them you are like a singer of love songs, one who has a beautiful voice and plays well on an instrument; they hear what you say, but they will not do it" (Ezek 33:32).

Then Jesus looks to the stony landscape of Palestine where rocks serve well for building a house's foundation. He metaphorically points to God as the ultimate bedrock as the Scriptures repeatedly note. For example, "The Rock, his work is perfect, and all his ways are just. A faithful God, without deceit, just and upright is he" (Deut 32:4), and "The Lord is my rock, my fortress, and my deliverer, my God, my rock in whom I take refuge, my shield, and the horn of my salvation, my stronghold" (Ps 18:2).[3]

Drawing upon this rich background, Jesus tells a story of two individuals: one who constructs his house on sand and another who builds on solid rock. During the stormy season a deluge takes place, causing flooding and results in the destruction of the house built on sand. Such events were not unknown in Palestine, with its contrasting dry and wet seasons, where an arid wadi could suddenly be transformed into a rushing current of water.

Jesus makes the connection between the foolish person who builds his house on sand with the person who hears his message but doesn't receive it into their lives. Conversely, the wise person who truly listens and acts upon Jesus's words is like the one who builds upon the rock whose house stands against the storm. The essential point in the narrative is the "doing and acting." As noted in Jesus's commentary, "Everyone who hears these words of mine and does not act on them will be like a foolish man who built his house on sand" (Matt 7:26). It is not enough to hear Jesus's words. They must be received and acted upon; otherwise, they have no lasting value. The wise person is prudent and sensible because she builds on solid rock. The one who builds on sand—not acting on Jesus's words—is foolish because the house's foundation is inadequate to stand against the storm.

How do the builders handle the storms that life inevitably brings? We know that the house needs to be strong if it is to withstand the blows from life's vicissitudes, and we also know that the people of God are not immune to life's turmoil simply because we have faith! We must center ourselves on God's love so that we can weather life's tempests.

Jesus walks with us every step of the way, ensuring that we do not face these challenges alone. Matthew affirms this very point as he relates another storm story. It is his well-known account of Jesus treading upon the water as the disciples' boat is battered about in a great squall. When his disciples first see Jesus, they are frightened. But soon Peter gathers his wits and recognizes it is the Lord and desires to go out to him. Receiving the Lord's consent, he amazingly steps out upon the water and walks towards

---

3. See also 1 Sam 2:2; 2 Sam 22:3; Isa 17:10.

Jesus, but is soon distracted by the waves and begins to sink. He cries out for help. Jesus catches hold of him and safely brings him to the boat while encouraging his little band to maintain their faith (Matt 14:22–33). Yes, Jesus travels with us throughout the ups and downs of our journey, but it is essential that we keep our eyes fixed upon him so as not to be overwhelmed by the unavoidable heartaches that life brings our way.

Knowing Jesus means that we not only hear his words but that we act upon them. A *laissez-faire* approach to Jesus and his instruction is not acceptable for a disciple of Christ. Rather, we are to participate in our relationship with Abba by working our spiritual muscles even as we work our physical muscles at the gym. While God gives us the great jewel of faith and empowers us by his limitless grace, he seeks our response of receptivity and gratitude. Indeed, our "yes" spoken in faith is both desirable and pleasing to God, ensuring our security. When the foundations shake, our relationship with Christ must be genuine or our spiritual house collapses due to the defects of its construction.

Building Successfully

Jesus is presented by Matthew as not only a great prophet to the nation of Israel, but also as the Messiah, the king of God's kingdom. (The Greek word "Christ" is the translation of the Hebrew word "Messiah.") This pronouncement of his kingship is first raised by the Magi in the nativity narratives (2:2). It is also affirmed by Jesus himself at the beginning of his public ministry (4:17). The teaching of the Sermon on the Mount serves as a summary of kingdom values and underlines the Christological focus of the gospel that Jesus is the Messiah of God.

A salient and essential question for us, then, is who is Jesus for us today? Is Christ primarily an excellent teacher who offers us life affirming values? Is he principally a fine role model whom we can pattern our lives after? Or, is he the King of God's coming kingdom and worthy of our devotion, commitment, and loyalty? If the latter, we need to ask ourselves if we insist on following our own agenda or are we daily recognizing him as our King? Is our prayer, "Your kingdom come. Your will be done?" Or do we reverse it to mean, "My kingdom come. My will be done?" The prime directive Jesus delivers to us is "to will one thing," as Kierkegaard has aptly noted. If we concur, then Jesus is worthy of our complete allegiance and unfettered energy.

Authentic Discipleship

A life committed to Jesus means that we do not settle for nominal discipleship. It asks us for more than lip service. Instead, it calls us to open our hearts to the Lord's leading and be enthusiastic in the service of our king. As highlighted in the text, the key word in Jesus's summons is *poieo*, or "acting, doing, or putting into practice," which suggests an active engagement in the rule of Christ. Ours is not to hear and forget his words, but to hear and do his words. We are not called to a loquacious outpouring of how much we love Jesus, but to an obedient engagement of listening and implementation of his words in our everyday experience.

As we noted earlier, Jesus emphasizes the crux of the matter is entering into a personal relationship with him implied in his dismissal of the "evildoers": "I never knew you; go away from me." As a result, we ask ourselves, "Do we *know* Jesus?" Is ours one of intimacy or simply talk and sleight of hand? As we have seen in this passage, the key for participating in God's kingdom is not religious jargon or mere rhetoric, but an authentic relationship between the believer and Christ.

Later in Matthew's Gospel, Jesus tells a parable featuring a man and his two sons while engaging the religious leaders (21:28–32). It goes like this: he asks one of his sons to go and work in the field. Initially the son refuses but finally complies. The father makes a similar request to his other son who, at the outset agrees, but later does not follow through and do the work. Jesus asks his listeners—who happen to be the chief priests and elders, "Which of the two did the will of the father?" To which his listeners correctly answer, "The first." Jesus's biting deduction is that the "sinners"—including people such as tax collectors and prostitutes—are entering the kingdom of God before his listeners, because they not only hear God's word but do it. These sinners surpass the endless chatter of the religious leaders who love talking, but not so much the doing.

As Jesus underscores this maxim, he notes that authenticity cannot be supplanted by charismatic exuberance. His interlocutors argue that they have accomplished mighty acts for God: "Lord, Lord, did we not prophesy in your name, and cast out demons in your name, and do many deeds of power in your name?" Their argument is passionate. They use the double vocative "Lord, Lord," while highlighting the amazing exorcisms and miraculous signs they have done. Amidst their barrage of words, Jesus simply listens. He does not deny their accomplishments; rather, he just waves them off, saying, "Stop bothering me! Whatever you have done, you have done.

But it has nothing to do with me. I don't even know you." No, enthusiasm is not enough. Fervor in worship is not enough.

What is needed is a true relationship with the triune God manifested in practical obedience. This changeless truth was announced by the prophets of old and beautifully affirmed with Micah's précis, "He has told you, O mortal, what is good; and what does the Lord require of you but to do justice, and to love kindness, and to walk humbly with your God?" (Mic 6:8). Signs and wonders, as impressive as they are, are no substitute for devotion and an acquiescent heart. What is needed is an authentic life expressed in gratitude, obedience, and compassionate love.

It is clear that following Jesus is not a once-for-all decision but a lifetime of saying "yes" to Christ, shaped by the qualities of persistence, perseverance, and radical stick-to-itiveness. It isn't for the faint of heart or those turned around by the latest fad, but for the brave of heart who continue to climb the mountain of faith regardless of challenges or stressors that threaten to waylay the upward path. To this end the apostle Paul urges us to keep putting off the "false self" and keep putting on the "true self," found in Christ and characterized by "compassion, kindness, humility, meekness, and patience . . . [and] above all love" (see Col 3:9–14). These are the virtues of the authentic life which mirror the divine image birthed in the garden of Eden, and which lie deep, hidden within our DNA. As we clothe ourselves with Christ we are transformed into his likeness and experience our own metamorphosis as persons created in God's image.

This process of conversion is enabled as we let go of our attachments, with all of their compensations and passing pleasures, and stay attuned to the Spirit's interior work, while unreservedly following Jesus as his disciple and friend. Moses models such an attitude by forsaking the pleasures and comforts of Egypt to listen to the voice of God (Heb 11:25–26).

A Daily Regimen

Authenticity is something that we all desire. We get tired of playing games, putting on masks, acting out roles—all for the purpose of impressing others and having our self-esteem assuaged. Such anxious striving indubitably wears us down and drives us to the precipice of despair. I believe that at our deepest levels we all desire to live authentically and this has been the case in every age.

Authentic Discipleship

I am reminded of the story of Saint Francis standing before his wealthy father Peter di Bernardone and the Bishop of Assisi, announcing his choice to serve God with a resolute and authentic heart. He declared it boldly by stripping off his fine garments, furnished by the wealth of his father, and standing naked before his inquisitors: "From this moment forth I am no longer Francis, son of Peter di Bernardone, but Francis, child of God."[4] By this animated gesture, Francis blazoned his profession to follow Jesus wholly, aligning himself with the poverty of Christ. He rejected the wealth and middle-class values of his father and embraced the honest and humble words of the gospel: "Blessed are the poor in spirit, theirs is the kingdom of heaven" (Matt 5:3). While we may not be called to follow the Lady of Poverty as Saint Francis, we all have our own God-given vocation. It is essential that we live it out in a genuine and uncompromising manner if we are to experience the joy, peace, and love of God's blessed kingdom.

To help us "walk the line" in such an authentic fashion, it is invaluable that we have a day-to-day regimen that supports our aspirations for spiritual growth. A necessary first step is to honestly assess our own inner condition. If we are going to make any changes interiorly we must see ourselves clearly and candidly; our inward gaze must be true or it is meaningless. Hence, a launching point for spiritual liveliness is to move forward from where we really are and not from an imaginary place of where we think we should be.

Second, we must listen for the Spirit's interior voice as the psalmist writes, "Be still and know that I am God" (Ps 46:10). It is essential that we take time to be attentive to God's voice every day and not always be jabbering away in our conversations with God. We are not always good at listening in our busy and frenetic lifestyle. Generally, we are a society of doers and not hearers. However, even as Elijah heard the "still small voice" amidst the storm (1 Kgs 19:11–13), so we must give ear to our Lord's gentle and humble voice. We need to stop our chatter and pay attention to the Spirit's intimate movements in our hearts and minds.

Third, we must all do our own deep-seated work. Paul makes this point in his letter to the Philippians when he says, "Work out your own salvation with fear and trembling" (Phil 2:12). No one else can do your inner work—not your parents, spouse, friends, or pastor. You must do it. You must climb your own spiritual mountain! The spiritual life does demand a certain degree of discipline. It is not a quiet walk in a secluded park. We must put in the labor for spiritual growth just as one develops skills in

---

4. Carretto, *I, Francis*, 11.

any other human endeavor. For example, if one is going to learn a musical instrument it requires many hours of practice; it does not just happen by thinking about it. In the same way, Jesus calls us "to put our shoulder to the plough and not keep looking backward" (Luke 9:62). Such a perspective encourages us to adopt a spiritual practice of intentionality and daily engagement.

Fourth, we must be patient with ourselves. There are going to be trip-ups, failures, letdowns—all part of the spiritual climb. It is not a steady ascent where we clamber up from one foothold to the next. No, there will be faulty steps, badly executed turns, and unforeseen slides. The key is to not give up; rather, take a long breath, get up, and begin again. Be patient with yourself, even as God is patient with you (2 Pet 3:9). Take tiny steps and keep moving forward a little bit every day. As the fable reminds us, the turtle wins the race and not the rabbit who runs rapidly but in a chaotic and disorganized manner.

Fifth, it works best to make one's spiritual pilgrimage in the confines of a community of faith. As we have seen, Jesus engages his ministry with a band of twelve disciples, and as his followers, we serve him best when we travel together. Indeed, as the apostle Paul reminds us, we both need and strengthen one another as "we are joined together and grow into a holy temple in the Lord" (Eph 2:21). The long and short of this is that we are not to give up on the church due to opposing perspectives or irksome personality traits that fellow believers manifest. To the contrary, we make spiritual headway when we work out our grievances together and doggedly pursue a spirit of unity and reconciliation as the people of God. It is in the resolution of these varied outlooks that we shine as a beacon to the world, demonstrating that love overcomes dissension and *shalom* forges friendship.

Finally, we can develop a daily "integral practice" to our spiritual regimen with elements that speak to all dimensions of ourselves.[5] For our body we participate in some activity that nurtures physical health like cardiovascular exercise, strength training, running, or walking. For our mind we study the Scriptures or engage in some other form of spiritual reading. For the soul we spend time in prayer or meditation. For our emotions we engage in worship, praise, or some other form of emotional release. The point is to involve each part of our person in a dynamic relationship with our triune God so that inner growth is cultivated in a wholistic, balanced, and harmonious fashion. When we do approach our interior formation in

---

5. See Marion, *Putting on the Mind of Christ*, 301.

this manner we find that there are contrasting doors we can open at any time that lead to devotional vitality.

We all have the capacity for embracing authenticity and living our lives truthfully. Regardless of our gifts and abilities, we are all invited to put on our true selves and become the persons that God envisioned "before the foundation of the world" (Eph 1:4). This process takes place by saying "yes" to God's charisma and staying true to our foundational calling throughout all of life's seasons. It is this commitment to say "yes" and the determination to repeat our "yes" that allow our development to unfold and become the true gift that our Artist God envisages. All of this happens by choosing—rather than non-choosing—that is, by continually making choices not to build on the shifting sands of egoistic desires, but rather on the firm foundation of Jesus's compassionate love.

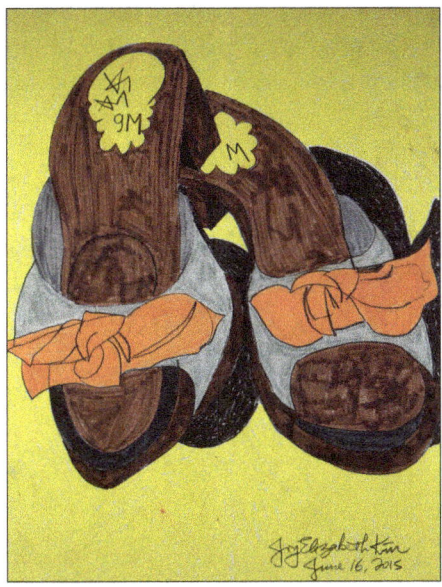

Questions for Reflection:

1. In your journal spend some time articulating what you mean by the word "authenticity." Why is authenticity something you value?

Part III: Moving to Maturity

2. The parable of building on the rock rather than shifting sand is one which makes sense. We know that rock provides a greater foundation than sand for the purposes of house construction. In what ways do you see yourself building your life on rock? Can you identify areas where you are building on sand? Reflect on these answers and pray over the details of how you are building your spiritual house.

3. Jesus's emphasis in this section of the Sermon on the Mount is upon "doing" the will of the Father and not simply "hearing" about it. Can you identify areas of your life where you are "hearing" but not "doing"? Can you see a way forward to change areas of "hearing" into practices of "doing" for the sake of God's kingdom?

4. Jesus uses the analogy of a tree bearing bad or good fruit. The tree bearing good fruit is cultivated while the tree bearing bad fruit is cut down. In what ways do you see yourself manifesting good fruit? Are there ways you are producing bad fruit? Spend some time journaling about these matters. How does this question of "bearing fruit" fit into your understanding of becoming a more authentic person?

Chapter 10

Salt and Light

Two Metaphors for the People of God

The world is cold. Someone must be on fire so that people can come and put their cold hands and feet against that fire. If anyone allows that to happen, but especially the *poustinik*, then he will become a fireplace at which men and women can warm themselves. His or her rays will go out to the ends of the earth.... Now, it is not I doing these things, it is Christ within me. My words are not my own. They are the echoes of God's voice that comes to me out of his silence. Now I know how to catch the fire from his words and become a fire myself, shedding sparks over the face of the earth. Now I can say that it is not I who live, but Christ lives in me.

CATHERINE DOHERTY

Poustinia, 49, 190

> *You are the salt of the earth; but if salt has lost its taste, how can its saltiness be restored? It is no longer good for anything, but is thrown out and trampled under foot.*
> *You are the light of the world. A city built on a hill cannot be hidden. No one after lighting a lamp puts it under the bushel basket, but on the lampstand, and it gives light to all in the house. In the same way, let your light shine before others, so that they may see your good works and give glory to your Father in heaven. (Matt 5:13–16)*

Part III: Moving to Maturity

THE ART PIECE OF Joy Kim's haggard army boots represents the challenges of simultaneously living in a "wild world" and living out our faith as both "the salt of the earth" and "the light of the world."[1] Kim's sketch reminds me of another artistic rendering, "The Christ of the Breadlines" by artist Fritz Eichenberg, which depicts Christ standing amidst a queue of homeless individuals waiting for a bowl of soup.[2] Eichenberg's wood engraving, originally used as an illustration in Dorothy Day's newspaper *The Catholic Worker*, expresses Christ's solidarity with the human condition even as Joy Kim renders the travails of the world in a pair of worn-out military boots. As Jesus expresses his compassionate heart to the wounded ones of our troubled planet, so we as his followers are to follow in his train as disciples of sacrificial love.

The metaphors of salt and light flow easily from the context of the Beatitudes which Jesus enumerates at the beginning of his Sermon on the Mount (Matt 5:3–12). The affirmations including "blessed are the poor in spirit," "blessed are those who mourn," "blessed are the meek," and "blessed are those who hunger and thirst for righteousness"—all express the upside-down worldview of the gospel which challenges today's contemporary mores of seeking power and coveting the preeminent position.[3] Conversely, Jesus encourages his followers to take up the role as *doulos*, or servant, which flows seamlessly from the values expressed in the Beatitudes. This perspective is vividly demonstrated in the Upper Room when Christ washes his disciples' feet, including Judas's, who is on the verge of betraying him (John 13). Such a selfless mindset is seen as Jesus looks into the eyes of his friends, reminds them of his love, and tenderly washes their feet, before sharing their final meal together.

In a similar way, as Christ's followers we are invited to be empathetic servants to those around us as we engage our day-to-day. The public at large may not believe that the *laos*, the people of God, have any role to play in a competitive society—indeed, we may be dismissed as being irrelevant or viewed as non-players in a fast-paced gig economy. Yet, as the community of faith we are called to shine forth as a lighthouse to a broken and hurting world, even as the Scriptures declare "that you may be blameless and innocent, children of God without blemish in the midst of a crooked and

---

1. "Wild World" is a song by Yusuf/Cat Stevens.
2. See Postema, *Space for God*, 169.
3. See Capon, *Kingdom, Grace, Judgment*, 15–25, for more on contrasting approaches to power, which he curiously coins as "right-handed and left-handed power."

perverse generation, in which you shine like stars in the world" (Phil 2:15). As we embrace our role as God's people, we portray the good news in word and deed, so that God's name is exalted and he is praised as Lord of the earth. Such a vocation is centered not on how we are feeling at any moment in time, but on Christ who is the merciful expression of the Spirit of God who breathes life and love over all of creation.

A Metaphor for the Church: The Salt of the Earth

Jesus continues his teaching on the mountain with the imperative "You are the salt of the earth" (Matt 5:13), which is a call to his band of disciples to look beyond themselves and recognize their mission to the world next door. The command stands in the second-person plural "you are," and as such, is not a private statement but is directed to the group at large. This image reminds both the disciples and the first-generation church ("you") that the focus is not simply to be inward, but that there is an outward imperative to address the needs of the broader community.

Looking more closely, we note that the image addresses three different spheres of penetration: it flavors, preserves, and purifies.[4] These modes of impact are exemplified both in the Old and New Testament Scriptures and provide a framework to understand the nuances of the "salt." For example, illustrations of the cleansing use of salt are found in the story of 1 Kings where the community of Jericho complains to Elisha the prophet about the quality of its drinking water. Elisha's response is to cast salt into it to sweeten it, and make it potable (1 Kgs 2:19–23). We also read in the New Testament of salt's refining work in texts such as "Have salt in yourselves, and be at peace with one another" (Mark 9:50) and "Let your speech always be gracious, seasoned with salt, so that you may know how you ought to answer everyone" (Col 4:6). These texts are examples of how the metaphor engenders both peace and gracious speech within and beyond the community of faith.

The external thrust of the church's impact is highlighted in the termination of the phrase "salt of the *earth*." The designation "earth" (*gn*) is translated variously as "soil, ground, shore, land, region, or earth." As such, the metaphor has a missional focal point which follows from Christ's earlier statement to his disciples, "Follow me, and I will make you fish for people"

---

4. Nolland, *Gospel of Matthew*, 212.

Part III: Moving to Maturity

(Matt 4:19). The disciples are to spread throughout the whole earth (*gn*) and communicate the life-changing values of the kingdom of God.

Drilling down deeper we observe another clue concerning the nature of "salt" in the subsequent statement, "but if salt has lost its taste, how can its saltiness be restored? It is no longer good for anything, but is thrown out and trampled under" (5:13). The key expression here is "lost its taste" (*moraino*), which is related to the English word "moron" or "fool." Literally, the Aramaic word for "lost its taste" means "become foolish" with the intimation that a foolish disciple has no effect on his or her sphere of influence.[5] The outcome of "being tasteless" is that if salt has no seasoning quality then it has no value and may as well be discarded. In this respect, it is unnatural for salt to lose its saltiness, even as it is anomalous for the believer to lose his or her distinctive flavour. Jesus's use of the metaphor implies the impartation of wisdom on the part of the faith community as it makes its way in the public arena.

The Sender sends his disciples out into the world to be an enlivening presence of wisdom and peace. We share in this mission as the "sent ones" of Jesus. We are not to settle for living quiet, comfortable lives while the world is caught up in unrest and agitation. Rather, we are called to be a people who bring *shalom* into a world where there is no *shalom*. Even as the crowds were amazed by the miracles of Jesus, as the Evangelist records, "When the crowds saw it [the healing of the paralytic], they were filled with awe, and they glorified God, who had given such authority to human beings" (Matt 9:8; see also 15:31), so the community of faith is to be a healing balm assuaging the pain of the world. This vocation is ours to claim so that we incarnate his compassionate presence in our everyday world. Our mission is both a great gift as we become his ambassadors to the world and a great responsibility as we represent the Lord of the Cosmos.

In our contemporary world the church needs to become "the salt of the earth" as it relates to the macro theme of caring for planet earth. If we are to be a purifying presence upon the earth, we must take our role of "tending the garden" seriously and with a measure of delight. As God gave to Adam and Eve the responsibility of "tilling and keeping" the garden, so we have the ongoing directive to care for our beloved planet. It is both unwise and irresponsible to live in our world in a "tasteless manner" where we give mere lip service to the health and well-being of God's created order. The church of God must not only be engaged in the process of planet care

---

5. See France, *Matthew*, 112.

but give leadership to this foundational practice. It is shameful when the church of Christ ignores or downplays its role in bringing *shalom* to our global home. Rather, we are encouraged to reclaim and own the truth that the psalmist boldly espouses: "The earth is the Lord's and all that is in it, the world, and those who live in it; for he has founded it on the seas, and established it on the rivers" (Ps 24:1–2). Our mandate of being "salt to the earth" rings out more "clearly, dearly, and nearly" as we follow Jesus with passion and give leadership to this foundational vocation of stewardship.

A Second Metaphor: The Light of the World

Jesus's second metaphor for his followers' engagement with the world has to do with light: "You are the light of the world. A city built on a hill cannot be hidden" (Matt 5:14). It is likely that the image's source is related to Isaiah's writings where the prophet references the ministry of the Servant of the Lord to the nations: "I am the Lord, I have called you in righteousness, I have taken you by the hand and kept you; I have given you as a covenant to the people, a light to the nations, to open the eyes that are blind, to bring out the prisoners from the dungeon, from the prison those who sit in darkness" (Isa 42:6). Similarly, we hear the prophet announce, "It is too light a thing that you should be my servant to raise up the tribes of Jacob and to restore the survivors of Israel; I will give you as a light to the nations, that my salvation may reach to the end of the earth" (49:6).

The salient point emerging from the new metaphor is that the disciples (and the incipient church) are to be a luminous light that cautions the surrounding culture of dangerous impediments while navigating life's perilous journey. In this way the community of faith serves as a beacon penetrating the spiritual darkness of a wild world. I think of the longstanding lighthouse off the point of Ucluelet, BC, warning ships of dangerous rock outcrops and providing a guiding light for ships to follow as they make for harbor. Indeed, the Ucluelet lighthouse casts its light seven miles out to sea and plays an essential part in the navigation of these treacherous waters. Without the aid of this lodestar the route is perilous and a high-risk venture to be sure if one makes for port after sunset.

As he did with the "tasteless salt" (Matt 5:13), Jesus follows this second image with an obvious truth—invoking the common Hebraic technique of parallelism—that one doesn't light an oil lamp and then hide its luminescence by "put[ting] it under bushel basket" (5:15). Doing so makes no sense at all! As is reasonable, one places the lamp on "a lampstand, and it gives light to all the house." We imagine a diminutive house of the first century with its one room, a modest window, and poor light. After sunset, the only illumination is a terracotta lamp placed on a lampstand providing a soft sheen of light. In my Bolivian travels I have been in numerous *casas de adobe* that are equally dark and in need of radiance from lamps or candles. In either context, it is nonsensical to put a lighted candle under a bowl; rather, one places it on the lampstand so that it brightens up the entire room.

Once again, we note that the image "You are the light of the world" presents the subject "you" in the second-person plural, indicating that the disciples, or the church collectively, are underscored as the world's light. Of course, this doesn't prevent individual disciples from shining as lights as well, but the focus is on the illumination radiating from the entire assembly. Together, the church enlightens society in a way single lights are not able to accomplish.

I remember diving the green emerald waters of Clayoquot Sound off the coast of Tofino. The waters darken quickly as one descends so a light is helpful as one descends to deeper depths. On one occasion I was diving with a British photographer who was doing a shoot for a magazine so he was employing some serious gear. As I had dived these waters before, I was down first and pulled out my light to peer through the forest-green waters. All of a sudden, the entire wall lit up from my buddy's sizeable lighting system used for filming in darker waters. As a result of the resplendent brilliance, I saw a myriad of red, orange, and green soft corals blanketing the walls, and to boot, a startled wolf eel swimming in the open water looking for a meal. Congruent with the light show was my singular impression, "Now that's a light!" Similarly, the collective body of Christ illuminates in a powerful manner the beauty of God's kingdom in a way which transcends the capacity of our lesser, but still important luminescence.

It is this combined presence of our individual lights shining forth within our personal spheres of influence and the collective light of the faith community which the apostles Paul and John argue make an impact on our surrounding culture. Their conviction is emphatic: "For once you were darkness, but now in the Lord you are light. Live as children of light—for the fruit of light is found in all that is good and right and true" (Eph 5:8), "so that you may be blameless and innocent, children of God without blemish in the midst of a crooked and perverse generation, in which you shine like stars in the world" (Phil 2:15); "For it is the God who said, 'Let light shine out of darkness,' who has shone in our hearts to give the light of the knowledge of the glory of God in the face of Jesus Christ" (2 Cor 4:6). Accordant with these texts is the verity that God himself "dwells in unapproachable light" (1 Tim 6:12) and as John writes, "God is light and in him there is no darkness at all" (1 John 1:5). To this end we hear the beloved disciple's appropriate admonition to the church of God concerning the light of Christ: "If we walk in the light as he himself in in the light, we have fellowship with one another, and the blood of Jesus his Son cleanses us from all sin " (1:7).

The Imperative to Be a Lighthouse

On the heels of the twofold imperative to engage the world as both salt and light, the Evangelist introduces a subtle shift in the second metaphor from "you *are* the light of the world" to "you *have* the light of the world." The light does not originate with us but is a reflection of the radiating light of Christ enlightening the world. As the moon isn't the source of its own light but reflects the light of the sun, so believers mirror the light of Jesus. The Gospel of John clearly articulates that Jesus *is* the light and does not merely have the light which illuminates the cosmos: "In him [*logos*] was life, and the life was the light of all people" (John 1:4); and "The true light, which enlightens everyone, was coming into the world" (1:9); "Jesus spoke to them, saying, 'I am the light of the world. Whoever follows me will never walk in darkness but will have the light of life'" (8:12). It is the light of Christ that we shine so that the world might know the peace, wellbeing, and abundance that flows from the person of Jesus.[6]

The outcome of the church radiating Christ's light is that society "may see your good works and give glory to your Father in heaven" (Matt 5:16). The directive is to live in a manner commensurate with Christ's light and to do so in the public arena so that people are drawn to his light. As we reflect Christ's light, we walk with people in the important work of sorting out life's fundamental questions of purpose, meaning, and vocation. Doing so, we help people to navigate inevitable obstacles, pitfalls, and challenges, and hopefully provide some assistance for a safe arrival home. The goal of this illumination is that we indeed become "children of light" so that the kingdom of God is manifested on planet Earth.

---

6. "Shine" in the Greek is *lampo*, from which we derive the English word "lamp."

Part III: Moving to Maturity

The dilemma we face is that there are opposing forces to the Christ light and we experience such a resistance interiorly. Part of us want to do God's will and part of us wants to go our own way. The apostle Paul speaks about this inner tension as he writes, "In their case the god of this world has blinded the minds of unbelievers, to keep them from seeing the light of the gospel of the glory of Christ, who is the image of God (2 Cor 4:4). Jesus mirrors this impasse in his conversation with Nicodemus: "And this is the judgment, that the light has come into the world, and people loved darkness rather than light because their deeds were evil " (John 3:19). The outcome for the disciple of Christ is, as Paul asserts, to "not give the devil a foothold" (Eph 4:27, NIV), but remain vigilant and attentive to the leading of God's Spirit so that Christ's light continues to shine brightly both inwardly and outwardly. There is urgency in the apostle's imperatives: "Put on the armor of light" (Rom 13:12) and "Put on the armor of God" (Eph 6:11), so that we will be able to stand "against principalities, against powers, against the rulers of the darkness of this world, against spiritual wickedness in high places" (Eph 6:12, KJV).

Jesus's entreaty to let our light shine is a trumpet call for action. It is not an appeal for a greater degree of rumination concerning the nature of light but a command to live our lives in a manner which gives glory to our Father in heaven. It is not about us receiving praise or adulation for being model citizens, but it is about God, the Ultimate Reality, receiving the glory due his resplendent name. Our job is to translate the mystery of God into expressions of *shalom*, in manifestations of unity, peace, joy, and selfless love. Christ only becomes "the light of the world" as we as individual disciples and collective body embrace our calling to be his instruments of light. The apostle John recognizes this reality when he describes the seven churches of Asia Minor as lampstands upholding and shining forth the Christ light (Rev 2–3). The crux of the matter remains that Jesus is the light of the world only when his followers reveal his light through actions of love, kindness, and mercy. There is no other way for Christ's light to shine upon the earth apart from the compassionate presence of his follower's luminescence.

This is the divine plan. We are God's partners in the establishment of his kingdom. It is his will that our participation matters. Evelyn Underhill reminds us of our essential vocation as coworkers in God's kingdom:

> We are the agents of the Creative Spirit in this world. Real advance in the spiritual life, then, means accepting this vocation with all it involves. Not merely turning over the pages of an engineering

magazine and enjoying the pictures, but putting on overalls and getting on with the job.[7]

Much depends upon our response to the Spirit's movement within our day-to-day lives.

The Implications of Being a Lighthouse

To begin, it is worth repeating that obeying the commands of Christ in what we do and say is essential service for the unfolding of God's kingdom. In spite of naysayers' denigration of the church of God, its efforts remain foundational for the proclamation and realization of Christ's ongoing work. The faith community both flavors and enlightens the world around it. It may be in bold colors, like church groups going to Bolivia to safeguard rural homes from the vinchuca bug which infects and causes the Chagas disease, killing thousands of people in Latin America every year. Or, it may be in ordinary actions, like buying groceries or doing errands for neighbors who are isolated in the COVID-19 pandemic. We must realize afresh that small stuff matters in the enactment of the spiritual and corporal works of mercy. Such deeds of mercy do not go unnoticed by our heavenly Father. As the writer of Hebrews reports, "For God is not unjust; he will not overlook your work and the love that you showed for his sake in serving the saints, as you still do" (Heb 6:10).

Second, kingdom living promotes a dynamic outworking of meaning and purpose. We see its opposite in today's culture. The precarious nature of self-worth on the psyche of the American worker exemplifies this lack of intention. Princeton economists Anne Case and Angus Deaton have brought to light in a recent publication the mental and emotional wellbeing of men and women without college degrees who have suffered badly in an economy where automation and outsourcing have left thousands of them unemployed and feeling unvalued.[8] Atul Gawande, who reviews the book for the *New Yorker* magazine, describes the impact of this new emerging economy on these jettisoned workers: "The work that the less educated can find isn't as stable: hours are more uncertain, and job duration is shorter. Employment is more likely to take the form of gig work, temporary contracting, or day labor, and is less likely to come with benefits like health

---

7. Underhill, *Spiritual Life*, 46.
8. Gawande, "Blight," 59–63.

insurance."[9] Furthermore, Gawande underlines the authors' discovery that the impact of such adverse economic factors have led to increased levels of drug addiction, suicide, despair, and a sense of hopelessness and helplessness.[10] In such a period of economic upheaval where purpose and meaning have been pauperized, the elevated mission of Christ offers a measure of solace, direction, and optimism urgently needed in these perilous times.

As we align ourselves with God's purposes we know that our lives matter and that we participate in the great work of creating *shalom* in our world. We are not simply numbers representing statistical probabilities on some bureaucratic dispatch, but valued persons created in the image of God. Together we receive gifts from the Lord of the universe who invites us to employ them for the redemptive purpose of establishing his bounteous kingdom. To this end we are all limitlessly loved by Abba and enrolled in his Great Work of recreating humanity and the cosmos. I believe it is fair to say that in our competitive and de-humanizing world it is all the more important to understand this bequeathment of personal worth.

Third, Jesus cautions us not to become sidetracked by secondary things as we take up our kingdom calling. He alludes to this possibility when he speaks about salt becoming tasteless or a lamp being placed under a bowl. To water down our enthusiasm for Jesus by pursuing our own middle-class comforts and conveniences is not a satisfactory approach if we are to take our discipleship seriously as followers of Christ.[11] Rather than distraction, we are to remain focused on what is essential. Our key practice is to stay centered on Jesus, and again, "keep willing one thing" as Kierkegaard put it in a previous epoch. Jesus's words are a call for action and not simply a call for more religious talk. To this end, our aim is to search out what is foundational, tune into the Spirit's work, and listen daily for her interior voice. As we show up, we know that Jesus shows up, and our relationship with him is cultivated, nurtured, and established. John the Evangelist underscores this enlivening relationship in Christ's words of consolation: "If you abide in me, and my words abide in you, ask for whatever you wish, and it will be done for you. My Father is glorified by this, that you bear much fruit and become my disciples. As the Father has loved me, so I have loved you; abide in my love" (John 15:7–9).

---

9. Gawande, "Blight," 62.
10. Gawande, "Blight," 60.
11. On this theme see Metzger, *Consuming Jesus*, 27–38.

Fourth, we are mandated with the task to live out the gospel in our everyday so that others may see our good works and give praise to God. Even as light pours through stained glass and displays the varied colors of the glassworks, so Jesus shines through us in the specifics of our personalities and talents. Each of us is uniquely gifted and express Christ's love in a rainbow of colors so that the richness of Christ is shown for all to see. I remember visiting the Hadassah Ein Kerem Synagogue in Jerusalem and being deeply affected by the stained glass windows created by the renowned artist Marc Chagall depicting Moses's blessings to the tribes of Israel. All of the rotunda's twelve windows present themes related to the specific blessing Moses spoke to each clan and are illuminated by a predominant hue. Together the windows create a vibrant dance of praise in a myriad of tones of joyful praise to God's enduring faithfulness to Israel. In like fashion, the nuances of our created persons and our spontaneous acts of kindness give expression to God's beauty and creativity so that he is magnified and adored.

Finally, as we manifest the light of Jesus, the manifold attributes of our heavenly Father are made visible for the world to behold. It is striking that it is in this context that Jesus first identifies God as "Father"—in Aramaic "Abba"—to his disciples (Matt 5:16). As Abba, our heavenly Father-Mother takes on the compassionate, nurturing role of a parent loving his or her little ones. Our Creator is not presented as a powerful, capricious deity like Zeus or Poseidon, seeking first his own desires, but as a loving Shepherd who cares for his children, as portrayed by Isaiah: "He will feed his flock like a shepherd; he will gather the lambs in his arms, and carry them in his bosom, and gently lead the mother sheep" (Isa 40:11). In equal measure, Jesus is described as the Good Shepherd who draws all of his children to himself regardless of which fold they presently find themselves on earth (John 10:16).

Through this amalgam of loving actions and relationships we make known the praiseworthy name of our triune God. We do so in a spirit of humility and dependence as we walk with Jesus throughout every season of our lives. To this end, we keep our eyes focused on our Savior who is the "author and perfecter of our faith" (Heb 12:2, NIV), even as Cardinal Newman penned,

Part III: Moving to Maturity

Lead, kindly light . . .
Keep thou my feet; I do not ask to see
The distant scene; one step enough for me.[12]

Questions for Reflection:

1. We considered salt's impact on its environment in three ways: flavoring, preservation, purification. As you live your day-to-day, are these effects apparent in your sphere of influence?

2. Jesus invites us to be "the light of the world" and to "let our light shine before others." He also suggests that at times we may hold back and prevent our lights from shining forth. In what ways are you letting your light shine out? Or conversely, are there ways you are dimming your light from the view of others? Spend some time reflecting and journaling upon these questions.

12. Newman, "Lead, Kindly Light," 1.

3. Ultimately, our words and actions are to be demonstrated in good works. As we fulfill our good works it gives praise to God and he is glorified. How does your conversation and behavior give glory to God and cause others to give him praise?

4. It is easy to become sidetracked and lose our spiritual fervor. When this happens, we become like salt that has lost its flavor or light that has been hidden under a bowl. A helpful first step in addressing this tendency is to identify and write down specific areas that trip you up in your following of Jesus. After identifying these obstacles, pray over them, and if possible, speak with a soul friend about these concerns.

Chapter 11

Turning the World Upside Down

Moving from Pride to Humility

Part of the realism of humility is its conviction that every one of us, being human, is prone to sin. We suffer congenitally from a weakness in the face of temptation, and a lack of purity of motives. This means we must watch ourselves and our motives. We must not allow ourselves to feel that we have "risen above" temptation, nor allow ourselves to be shocked when we meet sin in ourselves or others. Humility does not abandon its commitments; it does not indulge itself in the luxury of disillusionment. In short, it is humility that goes hand in hand with love, that makes love finally possible in such a jagged world as ours.

Roberta Bondi

To Love as God Loves, 55–56

> Then Jesus said to the crowds and to the disciples, "The scribes and the Pharisees sit on Moses' seat; therefore, do whatever they teach you and follow it; but do not do as they do, for they do not practice what they teach.
>
> "They tie up heavy burdens, hard to bear, and lay them on the shoulders of others; but they themselves are unwilling to lift a finger to move them.

Turning the World Upside Down

> "They do all their deeds to be seen by others; for they make their phylacteries broad and their fringes long.
>
> "They love to have the place of honor at banquets and the best seats in the synagogues, and to be greeted with respect in the marketplaces, and to have people call them rabbi.
>
> "But you are not to be called rabbi, for you have one teacher, and you are all students. And call no one your father on earth, for you have one Father—the one in heaven. Nor are you to be called instructors, for you have one instructor, the Messiah.
>
> "The greatest among you will be your servant. All who exalt themselves will be humbled, and all who humble themselves will be exalted." (Matt 23:1–12)

IN THE CULTURE OF SCUBA DIVING a favorite pastime is taking photos of the underwater world. It requires a fair bit of equipment as extra light is needed at depth to restore the natural colours lost from light's absorption. Depending on what the diver is planning to shoot, various lenses, light combinations, and even cameras are required to film the subjects correctly. For example, if one is filming tiny seahorses, certain macro gear is needed to capture their minuscule details but shooting schooling barracuda demands another approach altogether—including caution!

In a similar way, the Gospel writers put on a variety of lenses to present Christ at different times in his ministry to capture the specific nuances of his teaching. For example, in the Gospel of Matthew, Christ is often presented as the king of the coming kingdom of God who issues forth the necessary directives to inaugurate God's reign on earth (Matt 2:2, 11; 21:1–5). At other times, Christ is presented as the high priest who makes a sacrificial offering for the redemption of the people of Israel (20:26–28). And at others, Christ is depicted as a prophet who utters prescient words to the nation of Israel in need of guidance and direction (21:11, 46; 16:14, 24–26). It is in this role as prophet that Matthew portrays Jesus in his conversation with the crowds, scribes, and Pharisees in the text that lies before us in chapter 23. As God's prophet, Jesus speaks to the judgmental and self-centered attitudes of the religious establishment who advance a legalistic interpretation of righteousness and miss out on its core teaching—the way of humility lived in relationship with our compassionate God.

Matthew writes his Gospel to believers of the second-generation church. In this light it is imperative that they hear the prophetic words of Christ concerning the dangers of legalism, judgmentalism, and pride that so easily threaten the faith community when there is a jostling for power, status, and rank. In a similar vein, the church of Christ today faces the same destructive practices of our culture at large: a combative, divisive spirit; a rampant partisanship between political parties; and a complete lack of compassion for the stranger in our midst. The beauty of the scriptural pearl before us is that it not only prophetically critiques such damaging practices, but it expresses the core dynamic of what spiritual formation is all about: "All who exalt themselves will be humbled, and all who humble themselves will be exalted" (Matt 23:12).

A Critique of the Religious 1 Percent

Once more we find Jesus in the role of instructor as the crowds and his disciples gather around to receive his words. The Master Teacher begins by warning his listeners to be wary of the religious leaders who are offering counsel to the people. These doctors of the law are happy to claim the authoritative seat in the synagogue and instruct the people on the Torah's teaching but do not back their words up with a lifestyle pleasing to God.[1] Jesus summarizes his critique, saying (and I paraphrase), "Listen carefully to the Torah's instruction but do not follow the actual practices of these legalistic trainers." Jesus raises his listeners' awareness that instruction on the law is to be accompanied with a life fulfilling the ramifications of its teachings. It is not simply about delivering maxims so that one understands it, but a wholistic instruction comprising comprehension, practice, and personal devotion to it. Putting it bluntly, Jesus does not see the religious leaders practicing what they are preaching.

Moreover, Jesus argues that the Pharisees present an interpretation of the law which is out of step with its core intention. This misrepresentation includes a depiction of the good way as a laborious following of rules which is impossible to keep. The arduous nature of their instruction is indicated by the adage "They tie up heavy burdens, hard to bear, and lay them on the shoulders of others" (Matt 23:4). An example of such a burdensome approach is their observations on the sabbath which go far beyond the stipulations of the Torah (12:1-8). Such a punctilious detailing of the rules neglects the overarching truth that "the sabbath was made for humankind,

---

1. The reference to Moses's seat in verse two most likely refers to a chair placed at the front of the synagogue from which the teacher offered his commentary on the Old Testament Scriptures.

and not humankind for the sabbath" (Mark 2:27). Keeping the sabbath is meant to breathe life into one's walk with God and not be an enervating load discouraging heartfelt obedience.

In stark contrast, Jesus offers his description of the spiritual life as one where there is "rest for your souls" and an exchange of "heavy burdens" for a yoke which "is easy . . . and [one's] burden is light" (Matt 11:28–30). The paradigm of dividing one's life into an absolute set of rules and regulations misses out on the heart of the limitless love of God and places an onerous burden on the believer's back. Pursuing such a path more often than not comes from a desire to manage our relationship with God and control its final outcome by our own effort rather than experiencing the gracious gift of life located in the person of God's beloved Son.

Further, the religious leaders emphasize appearance rather than performance, as Jesus points out: "They do all their deeds to be seen by others; for they make their phylacteries broad and their fringes long" (23:5). In their scrupulous commitment to detail, the religious leaders take instruction intended to be helpful, and turn it inside out, to become expressions of pride and symbols of status. Specifically, the physical items of phylacteries and prayer shawls, meant to be devotional tools to help people remain mindful and centered in prayer, became symbols of pomp and circumstance used to impress the masses.[2] Furthermore, to have the freedom to pursue such rigorous practices required a degree of economic advantage that was beyond the capacity of the average citizen.[3] Such religious customs came to be seen as practices of class, wealth, and standing, rather than an honest attempt to have a closer relationship with God.

Such conventions most likely seem strange in our day-to-day world, but the desire to be known, valued, and esteemed by others is as real today as at any other point in time. Certainly, it is commonly understood that we are appreciated for what we do and accomplish in our utilitarian society. Hence, we, too, may attempt to distinguish ourselves in some way to create separation from the ordinary remainder of people.

Last, we read that the religious leaders loved to pull rank by insisting on the best seats at banquets and even when gathering at the synagogues. Such a desire for social standing led them to pursue honorific titles such as "rabbi," "father" and "instructor" (23:6–10). It is apparent that the religious

---

2. See Exod 13:1–10; Deut 6:4–9.
3. Keating, *Domingos en el Monasterio Mágico*, 161.

establishment desired adulation from the crowds and craved the esteem that their positions garnered.

Such aspirations are not unknown today and may even have some merit? Everyone likes to be appreciated for their service, even religious teachers and pastors. Nevertheless, to strive for position and power over others, securing the first place, is out of step with the gospel, for as Jesus says, "you have one teacher, the Messiah" (23:10). Recognition is one thing, but seeking rank over others within the assembly is unhelpful, and indeed damaging, for we are all equals as brothers and sisters. Such a pursuit of power signals our attraction to competition and hierarchy where we may fight one another for "more than enough" while others lack the basic provisions for living healthy lives.[4]

The Power of Humility

Jesus concludes his critique of the religious gatekeepers by offering a revolutionary alternative contained in the singular statement: "The greatest among you will be your servant" (Matt 23:11). This theme is obviously important to Matthew in his repetition of Jesus's emphatic instruction of servant leadership and lifestyle. Earlier Jesus answers the disciples' question about who is the greatest in the kingdom of heaven with the example of a little child: "Truly I tell you, unless you change and become like children, you will never enter the kingdom of heaven. Whoever becomes humble like this child is the greatest in the kingdom of heaven" (18:3–4). These are startling words when we think of it! Most often, children are intuitively aware of their lack of status in an adult world and venture forth with caution and instinctive deference.

Again, Jesus challenges his followers: "You know that the rulers of the Gentiles lord it over them, and their great ones are tyrants over them. It will not be so among you; but whoever wishes to be great among you must be your servant" (20:25–26). Authority in God's kingdom is established upon service rather than domination—not a pattern necessarily practiced in the political sphere or marketplace. Sometimes, unfortunately, it is missing even in the church. True leadership as understood in the Gospels is not forcing one's views on people responding to one's authority, but taking up the role of shepherd and graciously attending to the needs of others. It is

---

4. For more on the competing perspectives of "scarcity and abundance," see Palmer, *Active Life*, 121–38.

not a construct based upon "a power over model" but one of service and selfless love whereby the downtrodden are lifted up and those experiencing oppression are liberated. The epitome of Jesus's model of servanthood is demonstrated in the Upper Room as he kneels before each disciple, looks into their eyes, and tenderly washes their feet—including the eyes and feet of Judas, who is on the verge of betraying him.

The practice of service rather than the position of supremacy is the central motif of Jesus's instruction for the important role of helping others become fully human. The aspiration of being lauded by others is replaced with a realistic view of self—neither building oneself up or putting oneself down—but an honest self-appraisal not threatened by the success of others. In Jesus's paradigm for leadership there is the corollary statement, "All who exalt themselves will be humbled, and all who humble themselves will be exalted" (Matt 23:12). Humility becomes the underlying tone for the new way of doing things. Indeed, with Jesus there is a complete reversal of the world's pattern for doing things—to the degree that subsequent listeners identified his disciples with the backhanded compliment, "These people . . . are turning the world upside down" (Acts 17:6).

A Powerful Example

A compelling illustration of Jesus's perspective is found in Luke's parable of the Pharisee and the tax collector praying at the temple (Luke 18:9–14). In his prayer, the Pharisee reminds himself (and God) of all the good he has done through his righteous conduct and religious disciplines. He sees himself as an upstanding citizen, enjoying his prominence in the community. Meanwhile, off to the side stands a tax collector, despised by pretty much everyone due to his allegiance to the Roman regime and by lining his own pocket through excessive taxation. This man does not even raise his eyes to heaven, for he knows his own sin too well and simply mutters, "God, be merciful to me, a sinner!" Up to this point the narrative makes sense. A righteous man gives thanks to God while a derelict recognizes his own deep need for help.

The story turns on the subtle glance down the line when the self-righteous Pharisee compares himself with the down-and-outers, saying, "I am not like other people: thieves, rogues, adulterers, or even like this tax collector." As soon as the cleric compares himself with the wayward sinner, he engages in self-exaltation and experiences his fleeting reward (I feel good about myself. I am far better than this no-good charlatan!). In contrast, the tax collector doesn't compare himself with anyone else. He knows who he is. A sinner in need of mercy. The parable concludes with the surprising twist that it is the tax collector who goes home justified and not the sanctimonious minister.

The crux of the matter is that humility is the central ingredient for living an authentic life. It means that we are completely honest about who we are and what we have done. Humility doesn't play games. It is simple, even as its cognate, humus, refers to an ordinary lump of earth. A humble individual gladly prays: "This is who I am, Lord—with my faults in hand. Abba, I come to you openly and lean on your loving compassion. Lift me up and restore me to your ways of abundance and life." A lowly prayer is genuine. It reflects a teachable spirit that sees clearly the world—self, neighbor, and God. When we embrace humility, comparison and competition are not part of the equation. Rather, we engage the world and its inhabitants with loving compassion. As my Nigerian friend Olumuyiwa says, "There is enough room in the heavens for all birds to fly."

The virtue of humility lies at the core of our human journey because it mirrors our gentle Savior and his own downward path: "For the Son of Man came not to be served but to serve, and to give his life a ransom for many" (Mark 10:45). As meekness becomes a core value, then the aspiration for pre-eminence is replaced by a desire to nurture the well-being of others. It goes without saying that a spirit of docility and regard toward our home planet is also imperative so that all of God's creatures are respected, valued, and served. With this in mind it is no surprise that humility becomes the way forward in enacting the way of *agape* love, as Saint Paul reminds us in his letter to the Philippians, "Let each of you look not to your own interests, but to the interests of others. Let the same mind be in you that was in Christ Jesus . . . he humbled himself" (Phil 2:4–5, 8).

It's Not About Legalism or Status

Following Jesus is not about keeping rules but about nurturing our relationship with Abba. It is not about ticking off items on a celestial grocery list to ensure our standing before God. A legalistic mindset is decidedly not what knowing God is all about. Jesus makes this clear in his response to the Pharisee's question about the greatest commandment in the law. We know well Jesus's answer: "Love the Lord your God with all your heart and with all your soul and with all your mind" (Matt 22:34–37). The essence of the gospel is not captured by religious behavior but by a wholistic love for God. Jesus emphasizes this point in the Sermon on the Mount as he makes a series of comparisons (and I paraphrase): "It is true that we are not to murder, but don't forget about the more challenging bit of having an angry heart that leads to the violent deed" (Matt 5:21–22); "Adultery is indeed prohibited but do not neglect a lustful heart that leads to illicit actions (27–28); "Loving your neighbor is a beautiful thing but it isn't an excuse for hating your enemies" (43–44). Through these pairings (and others), Jesus asserts that a system of rigid rule-keeping doesn't penetrate to the deepest regions of our hearts; rather, we are to be open to the Spirit's interior movements, which impact every dimension of our lives. It is not about checking off points in our pharisaic notebook saying, "I don't do this, this, and this," and "I do do this." But it is about crying out to God as fragile, broken people who need Abba's inner healing, even as we see in the tax collector's desperate cry for the mercies of God.

Aligned with a rejection of a legalistic spirit is a corresponding veto on promoting our self-image at all costs. The Pharisees are all about self-aggrandizement, as illustrated in their desire for the best seats at the synagogues, places of honor at banquets, and salutations in the marketplaces. Their mindset is diametrically opposed to the approach of Jesus who doesn't give a whit about how others evaluate him but remains centered on the real needs of those he engages. Indeed, Jesus is critiqued by the religious establishment for hanging out with egregious sinners such as tax collectors and prostitutes, even to the point of eating meals with them! The story of Jesus dining at Simon the Pharisee's house and during dinner being anointed by "a woman of ill repute" is a case in point (Luke 7:39). As the woman lovingly sacrifices her precious alabaster oil, both she and Jesus are critiqued by Simon for the outlandish affair. In response, Jesus defends the woman's gracious and sacrificial gestures as those of a humble, contrite, and loving individual. The salient point is that Jesus is not worried about how his reputation will suffer from such a display of public affection. He recognizes that her actions flow from an authentic heart of wanting to know God more. In the same way, if we approach our day-to-day with the goal of keeping other people happy, we will likely miss out on our God-given vocation. Instead, Jesus invites us to meet with him daily, and in doing so, listen for his voice so that we are not waylaid by the neverending criticism of jaundiced onlookers.

Part III: Moving to Maturity

It's Not About Competition or Comparison

In tandem with Christ's focus on the true values of the kingdom of God is his robust commitment to the celebration of life over the pursuit of status, rank, and power. He isn't preoccupied by a spirit of competition and comparison. He has not studied at the best schools in Jerusalem or earned a PhD from an acclaimed university that he loves to parade about town. Rather, he is a young teacher from the cultural backwater of Galilee who enjoys being around society's outsiders and is happy to play with children whom he upholds as models for entering God's kingdom. Simply put, being at the head of the line is not his concern. His number-one goal is to celebrate the good news and lead others into a fulsome relationship with Abba.

We spend a lot of time and energy demonstrating how we are better than others and how we deserve the first place (or at least to sit at the head table). We waste copious amounts of effort fixating upon our fears and become increasingly agitated over our lack of deserved respect and recognition. Jesus simply doesn't go there. He expends his stamina and time traveling with friends (both men and women), enjoying good food, having a brew with his companions, and living an uncluttered life. At the same time, he is resolute about the concerns of God's bountiful kingdom. He is about celebrating the reign of God, not about bemoaning his standing among other well-known preachers. Ronald Rolheiser comments, "The most incredible and challenging of all Christ's teachings is that we can in fact be happy, that we can celebrate and enjoy life, even though we and the world we live in are far from perfect." Yet, he goes on plaintively to conclude, "Mostly we do not believe this."[5] I believe Rolheiser is right. Instead, as my daughter rues, we act like a Debbie Downer. We prefer the shadows of the human overcast rather than soaring above the cloud bank, while riding the winds of our prodigious and loving God.

It's Not About Judging One Another

Finally, as we discussed earlier, it is quite apparent from Jesus's words that we are not to judge one another but to embrace an attitude of repentance and humility. It is not our job to become God's constable on the lookout for failure and quick to press charges for every offence. One of the ingredients for such a judgmental attitude is a misguided perfectionism which sits at

---

5. Rolheiser, *Forgotten Among the Lilies*, 215.

the far end of the spectrum of self-awareness. We are not infallible, and it is unfair to expect it from our family, friends, or work colleagues. Instead, we are all broken individuals in need of God's healing touch. When we demand flawlessness, we hold individuals to an unattainable and unhelpful standard—one which causes others to become stuck in a spirit of pessimism and misplaced guilt.

We saw this attitude in the parable of the Pharisee who congratulated himself on his A grade while condemning the tax collector who couldn't scratch out a passing mark. Yet, it was the humble, abundantly realistic tax collector whom Jesus commended rather than the censorious Pharisee. Similarly, our critique of others only creates division and negativity. It hurts the ones we judge. It hurts ourselves. And it hurts our shared community. Ultimately, such a spirit is destructive, because at a foundational level, it negates the expression of compassionate love, which as Saint Paul reminds us, is the goal of the spiritual life (1 Cor 13). It is this sanctimonious spirit that underlines the pernicious characteristics of our day of racism, disregard of the poor, sexism, ageism, and an overreaching political partisanship.[6]

It's About Selfless Love

Jesus invites us to embrace his way of selfless love and to make it the foundation for our everyday living. None of us has it all together. None of us knows all of the truth. This is the reality of the human condition. Jesus simply encourages us to accept our limitations, live in humility, and do so in a spirit of love. No games. No competition. No comparison. Just receive God's love and pass it on. Perhaps, the pithy insight of Mr. Rogers' song "You've Got to Do It" can help us here.[7] For if we do it, we will know who did it, and this will help us to keep doing the beautiful work of Christ's compassionate love.

---

6. For more on the societal impact of judgmentalism, see Bondi, *To Pray and Love*, 109.

7. See the lyrics of Mr. Rogers's song, "You've Got to Do It," at http://www.neighborhoodarchive.com/music/songs/youve_got_to_do_it.html.

PART III: MOVING TO MATURITY

Questions for Reflection:

1. There is a tendency among religious people to reduce faith to a list of rules. Alas, as we have seen from our passage, this approach misses the fundamental point to develop a dynamic relationship with Abba. As you consider your own spiritual journey, can you identify dos and don'ts that come up for you on a regular basis which perhaps muddy the waters?

2. Jesus identifies humility to be a central component in our relationship with God and with one another. How do you understand humility and how is it apparent in your own walk with God?

3. Competition is useful in the world of sports as it helps to drive us to higher levels of success. However, comparing and competing with others for positions in the kingdom of God is not helpful at all. Spend some time journaling about the areas where you fall into the trap of competition and comparison. How do such tendencies impact your life negatively?

4. Jesus calls us to serve one another even as he served his disciples by washing their feet (John 13). How can you embrace the role of servant in your daily experience? Is it possible to do so while you are at work, at home with your family, or in your key relationships?

Chapter 12

Power of Duplication

Jesus called into existence a community of disciples to follow him at extreme risk. A safe Christianity is not genuinely Christ-like. Christianity will always be counter-cultural, a protest culture. And this means that we must always dare to stand up for what we believe in, to commit ourselves to our beliefs in spite of the tension between being a believer and belonging to the secular culture.

EDWARD FARRELL

Gathering the Fragments, 75–76

> *Now the eleven disciples went to Galilee, to the mountain to which Jesus had directed them. When they saw him, they worshiped him; but some doubted.*
>
> *And Jesus came and said to them, "All authority in heaven and on earth has been given to me. Go therefore and make disciples of all nations, baptizing them in the name of the Father and of the Son and of the Holy Spirit, and teaching them to obey everything that I have commanded you. And remember, I am with you always, to the end of the age." (Matt 28:16–20)*

THE DISCIPLES HAVE BEEN ENROLLED in the School of Christ for some three years. During this time Jesus has been teaching and modeling before them the ways and values of God's kingdom. Overall it has been a successful tutelage (with some bumps along the way), and they have made progress in their understanding and practice of the spiritual life. However, a new phase of ministry is starting up in which the disciples will be sent throughout the world with the message of God's redeeming love.[1] For this to happen, Jesus will no longer be physically with them, but will be with them interiorly as they announce the good news that "the kingdom of God has come near." It will be a new day—one which calls for attentiveness and discernment to the Spirit's voice. To this end, Jesus prepares them for their new roles as teachers, helping new students learn the values of God's kingdom.

Gathering at the Mountain

Following the stunning events of paschal week, the resurrected Christ informs his disciples through the women at the tomb to go before him to Galilee and he will follow soon and meet them there. Matthew identifies the location of the gathering as the "mountain to which Jesus had directed them," probably the hillside outside of Capernaum where Jesus had frequently taught both his disciples and the crowds—Matthew's collected material known as the Sermon on the Mount (Matt 5-7).

As the disciples arrive, the Evangelist notes that the group begins to worship Jesus, "but some doubted" (28:17). This amalgam of worship and doubt is not totally unexpected when we consider the astonishing events of the crucifixion and resurrection interweaving in such a remarkable fashion. Indeed, an honest valuation is that the journey of faith is always a combination of worship and doubt. Unwavering certainty is nigh on impossible as one climbs the spiritual mountain. It is not a sign of unbelief but simply a recognition that the pilgrimage of faith constantly brings new challenges that we must face and overcome. The answers are not always obvious. At times we are called to launch out into the unknown, and in faith, step out upon the water, as demonstrated by Peter. The reality is that some measure of doubt is always present, and on some days, we doubt more than we worship.

As we pay close attention to Matthew's wording of the closing of his Gospel, we are intrigued by his observation that the group sees Jesus from afar, making his way towards them. Matthew quietly observes, "And Jesus came" (28:18). Even as the resurrected Jesus came toward Mary Magdalene (and the other Mary) when they left the tomb, so Jesus approaches his disciples as they gather on the hillside. It bears similar characteristics to the story of Jesus coming alongside the two disciples making their way

---

1. Dylan, "Times They Are a-Changin."

toward Emmaus, as noted in the Gospel of Luke: "While they were talking and discussing, Jesus himself came near and went with them" (Luke 24:15).

As Jesus made himself known on those occasions, so he travels with us in our day-to-day. It happens in so many times and ways—if we have open eyes and receptive hearts to perceive his overtures. Indeed, this is what the life of discipleship is all about. It is about recognizing the serendipitous movements of Jesus. Jesus comes toward us, bringing his limitless love. He comes alongside us while we live our day-to-day. The good news is that we are never alone. Let us be ready to receive his touch and be receptive to the Spirit's revitalizing breath in our lives.

A good friend of mine once told me a story of making a spiritual retreat during a difficult time in his daughter's life. Throughout his time alone he was actively seeking God's discernment as it related to her challenges. Once while passing over a bridge and peering at the flowing waters below, he fixated upon a small branch that was caught up on its journey downstream. He kept watching the diminutive twig held up by the blockage in its way. Time after time the twig tried to get by, but it just couldn't free itself. Then curiously as if it received a slight push, it was free and made its way happily down the river. My friend whispered to me that God spoke to him through the seemingly inconsequential vignette of the branch's liberation: "Even as the branch became free after such a long struggle, so your daughter will be set free from the encumbrances that have burdened her for so long." While staring at the waters, my friend discerned the Shepherd's voice and knew the comfort of his presence. In a similar way, Jesus shows up in the everyday of our lives when we have the patience and awareness to recognize his compassionate presence.[2]

A Dynamic Challenge

Jesus comes to his disciples in a new way, no longer as the meek and mild Galilean teacher, but as the powerful and risen Lord of the reign of God. The quantum leap of breaking through the death barrier fully vindicates Jesus from the unjust attack on his character and mission by both the Roman regime and the religious establishment. Jesus speaks now as the risen Lord and addresses his disciples in the strength of this newly ordained position. "All authority in heaven and on earth has been given to me," he declares (Matt 28:18). His persona contrasts greatly with his quietude before Pilate

---

2. On discerning God's presence in all things see De Waal, *Finding God in All Things*.

(27:13–14) when he refuses to dialogue with the Roman governor. Now he plainly announces that the Father has bestowed upon him the ultimate rule of all creation, including the entire sphere of the heavens and of the earth. No longer is his focus limited to the nation of Israel, but he has put on the wide-angle lens, which includes the entire earth and the vastness of the heavens.

God's magnificent power as demonstrated in Jesus's resurrection is the "Divine Yes" to the ministry and personhood of Jesus. He is the faithful "Son of Man" who has shown obedience and sacrifice at every stage of his spiritual journey, and as such, is crowned King of God's new kingdom. The glory which we see bestowed upon the resurrected Christ resonates well with Daniel's vision foreseeing a new work of God upon the earth when he prophesies,

> I saw one like a human being coming with the clouds of heaven. And he came to the Ancient One and was presented before him. To him was given dominion and glory and kingship, that all people, nations, and languages should serve him. His dominion is an everlasting dominion that shall not pass away, and his kingship is one that shall never be destroyed. (Dan 7:13–14)

As the newly crowned King, Jesus's first directive to his disciples is the imperative "Go into all the world" (Matt 28:19). Here he entrusts them with the charge to be his representatives throughout all the world. The order is meant to encourage and challenge his disciples that they have a substantive, ongoing role to play in the unfolding reign of God. Even as Abraham received the call to leave Ur of the Chaldees and go out to an unknown country and Moses heard the message of God from the burning bush to go to Pharaoh and tell him to "let his people go," so the disciples receive Jesus's manifesto to go and proclaim the good news to all the nations. Jesus is the Sender and the disciples are the sent ones and they are to go out and speak "the word of his [God's] grace" (Acts 14:3).

In a similar way, Jesus sends us out today to speak his message of compassionate favor. It is a word of love, joy, and peace—one which our broken world so badly needs to hear. It is not about critiquing or judging folk, but simply telling people of God's amazing grace which covers all of our shortcomings. Where we often struggle with issues of purpose and identity, Jesus reminds us of our fundamental vocation which is to be his "sent ones" and communicate the life-changing story of God's compassionate love. We have a purpose, and it is an essential one; take up our part and add our stitches to the tapestry that the Spirit is so beautifully weaving.³

A Call for Duplication

Jesus's commission begins with the dynamic call for his followers to go out into all the world and make disciples. Since the Greek word for "disciple" is etymologically related to the noun "learner," people are not invited to become casual listeners but committed followers of Jesus. It is not enough to become converts to Christianity. The expectation is to become mature Christians who engage in the hard work of serious discipleship. The invitation is to not become baby believers but adult companions of Christ. The summons is for us all—not limited to a spiritual elite who alone muse on religious things. We all receive the divine overture to become both disciples of Christ and disciple-makers so that God's kingdom flourishes throughout his resplendent creation.

Jesus demonstrates this divine overture in his interaction with the woman at the well in John 4. He reveals to her that he is able to provide "a spring of water gush[ing] up to eternal life." Without hesitating, she quickly responds, "Sir, give me this water, so that I may never be thirsty or have to keep coming here to draw water" (4:14–15). Her receptive spirit to Jesus's invitation is shown in her determination to go and tell her friends so that they can come and take in his words of life. Here we see the Samaritan woman's choice to follow the path of discipleship in spontaneous witness of her transformation.

The command to go and make disciples is a challenging vocation. It is a path that requires persistence and patience and one that is costly (Luke 14:28–30). It isn't easy. It is a way of self-denial and carrying one's cross (Matt 16:24–26)—even as Jesus carried his cross to Golgotha. The work is slow—even as our Father in heaven is a patient and slow God. The psalmist writes, "The Lord is merciful and gracious, slow to anger and abounding in steadfast love" (Ps 103:8). Similarly, we are encouraged to replicate God's long-suffering love as we travel this path ourselves, assisting others in making their fundamental journey. Our goal is to walk beside them throughout the seasons of life and help them to know and experience God's compassionate love. This approach of making soul friends is a one-person-at-a-time

---

3. See Underhill, *Spiritual Life*, 51–52, for more on the church's purpose cooperating with the Spirit to "save the world."

effort. It is not a mass movement. Each person makes their own decision for Christ. Following Jesus requires persistence and intentionality in real time. It is not an on-again/off-again relationship due to the fleeting moods of the day. Rather, it consists of tiny steps of faithful living where we embrace Jesus in the everyday of our lives.[4] When we help people repeat their "yes" amidst the storms of life, we aid them in the essential work of authentic discipleship.

The Step of Baptism

Making disciples includes the bold step of following Jesus in the waters of baptism. Jesus introduces the critical nature of this directive with the trinitarian formula, "baptizing them in the name of the Father and of the Son and of the Holy Spirit" (Matt 28:19). He does not use it as a philosophical statement to be bandied about by zealous seminarians, but as an invitation to join the loving conversation between the persons of the Divine Family. The image is relational. It signifies entering a dynamic relationship with the triune God as beloved daughters and sons.

The nuances of the heavenly family are imagined beautifully in the film *The Shack* as Father God is depicted as an affectionate African-American matriarch, the Holy Spirit as an attractive young millennial Asian woman, and the Son as a robust young man of Middle Eastern origin. Throughout the piece the trinitarian family is presented as a warm, loving household with much laughter and joy. In my mind it evokes well the intimate fellowship that we as God's children are invited to enjoy as part of the *laos* of God.

As Jesus was baptized in the Jordan River by John the Baptist and heard Abba's voice say, "This is my Son, the Beloved, with whom I am well pleased" (Matt 3:17), so we are to follow Jesus and through baptism express our loyalty to the Father. This truth was echoed in Jesus's transfiguration on Mount Tabor when the disciples heard the voice of God say, "This is my Son, the Beloved; with him I am well pleased; listen to him!" (17:5). The closing imperative from the Father, "Listen to him!" highlights the crucial nature of paying attention to Jesus's commands and expressing our full commitment in saying "yes" to his word.

Jesus's baptism was a public event expressing allegiance to his Father's will. In a similar way our own step of baptism is to be a public act in which we openly make our confession of faith. Through it we become witnesses to

---

4. See Yaconelli, *Messy Christianity*, 127.

the saving work of Jesus and to the fact that our primary loyalty is to him, superseding any other competing demands. Baptism is not a cold, formal rite which we undertake due to catechismal regulations, but an intentional step of embracing the intimacy of Divine Love. It is not due to ideological demands but a chosen response of saying "yes" to Abba's affirmation that we are his adopted sons and daughters. As Jesus is the Beloved of God, we also become his beloved children and friends of our tenderhearted Savior.

Baptism is a telling sign that we participate in the community of Jesus, as expressed in the rich Greek word *koinonia*, which is normally rendered as "community" or "fellowship." It is a designation which contains the complementary ideas of "having a share in Christ" and "giving a share of Christ" which underlines Jesus's ongoing presence within us and our participation in his risen life. Through our participation in the body of Christ (the church) we share in a loving community which supports us as we make our spiritual journey amidst the vicissitudes of life. Moreover, we participate in the global people of God, empowered by the Holy Spirit, and demonstrated by its rich movements of diversity, inclusivity, and vitality. We are not alone. We are members of an international community living out the values of our Leader as expressed through the fruit of the Spirit—"love, joy, peace, patience, kindness, generosity, faithfulness, gentleness, and self-control" (Gal 5:22–23).

The Weightiness of Teaching

Making disciples includes helping potential followers to understand what the kingdom of God is all about. Even as Jesus taught his own band about the values of God's kingdom, so they—and we—are to pass these principles along to others. This new practice of teaching is to be done in a demeanor of humility, love, kindness, and patience. Disciple-makers go out not as an occupation force, but as peacemakers who represent the Prince of Peace. In a likewise fashion, our contemporary mandate is to assist others to understand both the written word of God and the Living Word as manifested in Jesus Christ, God's Son. As Jesus underlines in his departing declaration, "teach[ing] them [new disciples] to obey everything I have commanded" (Matt 28:20), we recall that the verb "to obey" is used in the sense of "to hear" or "to pay attention." Obedience is not about remembering hundreds of rules, or passing an exam, or receiving a good grade. Rather, it involves listening to the compassionate voice of the Holy Spirit and following her guiding hand in the gist of everyday life. We listen for the Spirit's voice because we understand that her will for our lives is always shaped by goodness, love, and beneficence. Our triune God is not interested in deprivation, like a grim reaper or a scrooge, but like a loving mother who blesses us with "grace upon grace" (John 1:16).

Teaching people about who Jesus is and what it means to follow him takes time. It cannot be rushed. Even as fruit grows slowly, it takes time for the seed of faith to mature in a fulsome manner. For this to happen, the burgeoning fruit must remain attached to the tree; the disciple must remain connected to the community of faith to gain spiritual maturity. The coupling between teaching and discipleship is most effective when done in the context of the body of Christ. As we learn and grow collectively, we help each other become all that Jesus envisions. Discipleship is not a solitary path, but a group effort as we walk in solidarity with the bountiful body of Christ. As Bonhoeffer writes, we are to live our "lives together" and by doing so we follow in the footsteps of Jesus who established the first Christian community in his intimate band of disciples.[5]

Jesus's emphasis here on "teaching" (*didasko*) is new. Up to this point he has been the teacher and the disciples have been his students. But now he is passing the instructor role on to them, and they in turn are to pass it on to others. Jesus is ascending to the Father but in a short time he will send the Holy Spirit to empower them (and us) in the crucial work of teaching others. Hearing Jesus's words we also have confidence that we are able to understand the biblical truths and faithfully pass them along to new believers.[6] It is not enough simply to feel good about coming to church and having an uplifting worship experience. Rather, spiritual substance is the goal and this comes about through a faithful practice of hearing and doing the words of Jesus. As such, it is imperative that the faith community considers the ways in which the core elements of the faith are transmitted to all of its constituents (including children and youth) and be faithful and intentional in all dimensions of its communication.

Maintaining a robust relationship with God is crucial, but it is not the last word in the important work of renovating our minds in Christ. Paul reminds us that we are to put off the mores of our culture. We must not construct our personal identity on our culture's values but transform our

---

5. See Bonhoeffer, *Life Together*.

6. See 2 Cor 3:5–6 on the competence that God gives us to faithfully transmit the gospel to others.

minds by putting on the mind of Jesus (Rom 12:1–2). For this transformational work to take place we are enjoined to immerse ourselves in God's word within the context of his body, the church, so that we experience the ecclesial support that is needed for such a radical change. To accomplish this metamorphosis, there is an urgency within the contemporary church to reassert the centrality of preaching and the reading of Scripture within the worship experience to establish a firm foundation for spiritual fruitfulness. Funny stories, pleasant feelings, and even enthusiastic praise are insufficient in themselves for establishing the requisite bedrock of faith when the foundations of our culture shake.

A Farewell Promise

Jesus's last words before ascending to the Father is the comforting declaration, "And remember, I am with you always to the end of the age" (Matt 28:20). Recognizing that his final instruction may seem daunting, Jesus reminds his disciples that he will be with them through his indwelling Spirit in every situation they encounter. Rather than overwhelming his disciples with an impossible command, his words become a source of motivation. His consoling presence will never leave them. Indeed, he emphasizes this point as he employs the first-person pronoun "I" (*Ego*) am with you always." His presence with them remains unbroken. Jesus will never leave them alone. Nor does he leave us alone, as we participate in the work of his kingdom. His name remains "Emmanuel," as the angel of the Lord told Joseph at the beginning of Matthew's Gospel: "they shall name him Emmanuel, which means 'God is with us'" (1:23).

The promise embedded in the text—at the beginning of Matthew's Gospel and at its end—is that we can count on Jesus's everyday companionship—in every circumstance, in every situation, in every trial. He walks beside us as Teacher, Lord, and Friend. Jesus's final words are meant to encourage, embolden, and empower every generation of believers to take up the vision of becoming passionate disciple-makers for the kingdom of God. As such, we are not to drift aimlessly through life, daydreaming about bygone days, but to go forward resolutely in the enlivening work of serving the *Kyrios*, Lord of the Universe, "so that at the name of Jesus every knee should bend, in heaven and on earth and under the earth, and every tongue should confess that Jesus Christ is Lord, to the glory of God the Father" (Phil 2:10–11).

Part III: Moving to Maturity

The challenge we face is to remain attentive to Jesus amidst the storms of life. It is all too easy to become distracted and tossed about by the vicissitudes of life (Jas 1:6) so that our focus is waylaid by the storms' rollers and we lose sight of the Pilot of our souls. It is no accident that a common artistic rendering for the church in the first centuries was a ship being pummelled by storm breakers. The same thing happens today. We travel together in the ark of the church, tossed about by life's hurricane forces; but the Master remains with us, enabling our safe arrival home.

It is imperative that we stay attentive to Jesus's indwelling presence as we live in our everyday. To assist us here we have the spiritual disciplines of silence, solitude, and prayer (amongst others) to help us remain alert to the Spirit's interior succor. A beneficial practice is to begin each day in time spent with Jesus so that we enter it in a mindful and equanimous spirit rather than a dazed lethargy of spiritual stupor. Try not to rush into your day. Draw apart—even for a few minutes. Slow down. Breathe. Calm your mind. Hear Jesus's encouraging voice, "I am with you always." Then enter into the day unfolding before you.

"Forwards!" Not "Backwards!"

Jesus does not promise that we will experience success at every turn but he does promise to travel with us and give us a purpose in living that is both rewarding and meaningful. He is the Sender and we are the sent ones so let us get on with the job of sharing the good news of Christ's life, hope, and joy. At a recent exhibition at the Ontario Art Gallery entitled "Impressionism in the Age of Industry," I took pause as I watched Lumière's black and white silent movie (filmed in 1895), depicting the doors of the Lumière factory opening wide in Lyon, France. It is a simple, direct shot capturing the moment when the workers pour out of the factory at the end of their shift—mostly, young women attired in long, modest gowns, a few men on foot or bicycles, two or three dogs winding their way through the exiting mass, and surprisingly, a horse and carriage for good measure! Like waters gushing forth from a cracked water main, the workers spew out of the yawning factory gates all in a rush to get on with life's more pressing goings-on.[7]

What impressed me in this viewing was the realization that every person in the film died long ago. No one remains. Women, men, dogs, horses—all gone. Every young person walking briskly through the wooded

7. Lumière, *Exiting the Factory*.

doors of the Lumière factory—with all of their hopes, plans, and aspirations—has completed their journey of life. My thoughts turn to questions like these: What happened to them? Where are they now? Were some of them followers of Jesus? Do they rest now in Abba's compassionate arms?

The film short presses my mind in the direction of what theologian Paul Tillich calls "ultimate concerns."[8] An example of such a "concern" is the nature of our fundamental vocation and what provides meaning for our human journey. Keeping this in mind, we hear again Jesus's divine imperative "to go and make disciples of all nations . . . teaching them to obey everything that I have commanded you." Can we hear afresh that the Sender sends us out into his world to communicate the life-changing truth that "the Kingdom of God has drawn near"? This is the good news that we are invited to proclaim both in word and deed—Jesus Christ is Lord of all creation, and the tectonic truth that "it is Abba's good pleasure to give you [us] the Kingdom" (Luke 12:32).

It is worthwhile to consider whether we are doing all we can to help people know the love, grace, and mercy of Jesus. In my roles as professor and pastor, I am impressed with N. T. Wright's article in a recent journal which includes the following question to seminary professors: Are you helping your students fall in love with the biblical text?[9] In this piece Wright argues that it is not enough for the Scriptures to be presented solely on an information level; rather, it is essential that the biblical truths be explored in an inspiring fashion so that the students' hearts and minds are piqued within them (Luke 24:32). We can add that the same suit applies to clergy speaking from their pulpits, Sunday School teachers instructing their classes, or individual Christians sharing with their work colleagues. Of course, it is not limited to a conversation about the sacred text but opening our lives up in an authentic manner which resonates with the words of Jesus. When we do this on an order of both word and deed our witness rings true, causing hearts to stir and spirits to turn to the Divine Heart of limitless love.

---

8. Tillich, *Dynamics of Faith*, 1.
9. Wright, "Home in the First Century," 14.

Part III: Moving to Maturity

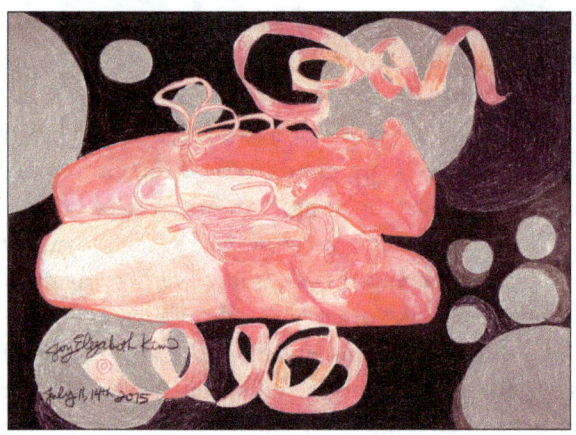

Questions for Reflection:

1. Jesus is the Sender and we are his sent ones. He calls us to go out into our world and through word and deed communicate his compassionate love. As you reflect on Jesus's invitation consider the ways you can help others grow in their faith. Are there specific steps you can take to come alongside others and assist them in their spiritual journey?

2. In his final mandate Jesus highlights the important area of teaching in the process of making disciples. In my experience I have seen that many churches have opportunities for people to use their teaching gifts in the areas of adult, youth, or children's ministries. Is it possible that you could teach in one of these capacities? Spend time praying over this vital area of service so that the Spirit will raise up teachers (you or someone else) for the maturation of his church.

3. Mentoring others is an excellent way to engage in the ministry of disciple-making. It happens as we spend time with new believers and help them to understand and grow in the ways of Christ. Take time to reflect and journal about how you might walk with someone as a spiritual companion.

4. Participating in a cell group has proven to be a wonderful way of both growing and helping others to grow in their walk of faith. Consider the ways you might participate in a cell group as either an active participant or as a group leader. Know that your involvement in a discipleship group will pay dividends for your own spiritual growth and for the enrichment of others as you walk together in Jesus.

Epilogue

THE IMPERATIVES OF JESUS call us to take his words seriously and to demonstrate our commitment by incorporating his teaching into our everyday lives. I have identified this intention of declaring our "divine yes" through the caption "walking the line." We are to walk the line by listening, choosing, and implementing the enlivening words of Christ in our daily experience.

The apostle Paul addresses the same thought through his use of the Greek word *stoicheo*, which means "to be in line with," "to follow," "to hold to," "to conform to," as illustrated in the following passages: "Only let us hold fast to (*stoicheo*) what we have attained" (Phil 3:16); "If we live by the Spirit, let us be guided (*stoicheo*) by the Spirit (Gal 5:25); "As for those who follow (*stoicheo*) this rule—peace be upon them, and mercy, and upon the Israel of God" (Gal 6:16). In these examples, *stoicheo* depicts a line of people keeping in step with one another like soldiers marching in rank and file, or simply an individual following in someone's footsteps. We are to track the footsteps of Jesus in a spirit of commitment, discipline, and enthusiasm.

In one sense, it is a challenge to live for Jesus with both a passionate and disciplined spirit. Our commitment to pleasing ourselves often trumps our higher calling and waylays our efforts to climb the spiritual mountain. What we do know is that to have any success in our spiritual pilgrimage, we must stay close to Jesus by daily feeding on his word and breathing in his empowering Holy Spirit. Jesus uses an image that illustrates this enlivening dynamic in his Upper Room discourse with the disciples in John's Gospel: "I am the vine, you are the branches. Those who abide in me and I in them bear much fruit, because apart from me you can do nothing" (John 15:5). Branches only thrive as they receive the flowing sap from the main vine. Without the energy from the mother vine, the branches inevitably dry up. In a similar way, we must draw strength from Jesus, for he is our ultimate soul food and constant source of spiritual nutrition. The good news is that

Epilogue

as we stay connected to Christ, he enables us to "walk the line" and live lives of fruitfulness and abundance.

Alas, our lives are a mixture of ups and downs even on the spiritual front. The disciples did not know continuous success but carried their share of questions, doubts, and failures. So with us. We congruently experience competing emotions and aspirations at various levels of our consciousness. At the surface we may be going through a ferocious trial, but at an interior level experience the tranquility of God's restful hand. The key to remember is that the mélange of repose and turbulence is not a sign of spiritual immaturity but an indication of the complex nature of our human condition. Of course, at times we intensify the oscillation by dabbling in the gods of our world—comfort, security, power, money, pleasure, entertainment—and these invariably create unnecessary tension and upheaval. We imitate Rachel of old who stole the family gods by hiding them under her camel saddle when fleeing from her father Laban. While Jacob was obeying God's call to return to his ancestral home it seems that Rachel was slow to forsake the gods of her youth and by her sly hand came an inch away from an untimely demise (see Genesis 31 for the full story). Similarly, we bring upon ourselves many interior and exterior encumbrances with our infatuation with the totems of this world, regardless of the alluring names they bear.

The good news is Abba is aware of our proclivity to error and remains committed to us in spite of our fragility. The prophet Jeremiah captures this divine empathy by depicting God as the potter working away in her pottery. She works the clay at her wheel, kneading, shaping, and forming it—carefully pressing it into its desired shape. Despite her care, the clay periodically breaks apart due to its delicate nature; yet, she doesn't discard it but continues to mold it until it becomes pleasing to her eyes (Jer 18:1–6). Similarly, Abba works the clay of our lives, molding us into the image of his Son, never giving up on us despite our cantankerous attitudes, rebellious spirits, and self-seeking ways. God is so, so, good to us. He never forsakes us even when we are screaming mad and deliberately making choices that hurt ourselves and others. Our Creator God perseveres as the Master Artist who loves the exquisite pieces she is fashioning and bringing to fruition. Thankfully, Abba loves us with a boundless affection that catches sight of the entire canvas, not waylaid by the quirks of the clay.

The vision of God as revealed in his Son Jesus is a mind-blowing, transcendent juggernaut! His purposes outstrip our creative capacity, and as a result, make it difficult to ascertain and follow by our own efforts. We

Part III: Moving to Maturity

simply can't do it on our own. It is imperative that we depend on the Spirit of Jesus at every turn if we are to know the truth of God's kingdom. The "Jesus Project" is beyond our imaginative wherewithal as Carlo Carretto highlights, "Who could have understood the 'Jesus Project', in which victory is won by losing, in which the believer's strength lies in his weakness (cf. 2 Corinthians 2:9–10), in which happiness resides in poverty and powerlessness, and death is gain (cf. Philippians 1:21)?"[1] Only by the energy of the Holy Spirit are we able to say "yes" to Jesus's imperatives and to the upside-down world of the Gospel's Beatitudes.

Allow me to end this monograph with a personal story. As we have all experienced, the COVID-19 pandemic has played havoc with our daily regimen. For me, it has been difficult and at times impossible to get to the gym and work out. As a creature of habit, I miss this regular routine of working out to reduce stress, improve my cardio, and fend off the onslaught of shortening cerebral synapses! My go-to alternative is to go down to the basement, ride the exercise bike, do lunges along the hallway, and use my eight-pound dumbbell for easy-goes-it resistance training. However, the most helpful addition in my new training program is the use of a Pilates roller. If you aren't familiar with it, don't worry. Most folk have never heard of it. It is simply a hard foam roller which a person lies on to massage the back and activate one's core. The challenge is to maintain your balance on the roller while doing different movements, for example, lifting alternating arms and legs. As you do this your core strengthens, improving posture, muscle tone, flexibility, and body awareness. The key is to do all the exercises while not falling off the roller. It is all about balance.

Balance is critical in the exterior and interior worlds. It remains at the very core of God's mysterious kingdom. Paul alludes to it when he speaks of God "working in us for his good pleasure" while "enabling us to do our part" in the tapestry the Spirit is weaving (Phil 2:13). This divine-human partnership reminds me of finding my equilibrium while lying on the wobbly Pilates roller. I have to work with the roller so that my core resonates with its subtle movements so I am not jettisoned unceremoniously to the floor. Similarly, we are invited to maintain our connection with Jesus while listening for his voice amidst the tremors of this rocking world. "Walking the line" is about maintaining our interior balance while engaging body, mind, and spirit for the renovation of our world. May we steady ourselves by holding on to Jesus who invites us to become both his coworkers and

---

1. Carretto, *I Sought and I Found*, 120.

Epilogue

soul friends, destined to enjoy his timeless companionship and unfading affection.

Bibliography

Abraham, K. C. "A Theological Response to the Ecological Crisis." In *Theology: Voices from South and North*, edited by David G. Hallman, 65–78. Maryknoll, NY: Orbis, 1994.
Barth, Karl. *The Epistle to the Romans*. London: Oxford University Press, 1968.
———. *Evangelical Theology*. Grand Rapids: Eerdmans, 1963.
Bettenson, Henry. *Documents of the Christian Church*. Oxford: Oxford University Press, 1963.
Bondi, Roberta. *To Love as God Loves*. Philadelphia: Fortress, 1987.
———. *To Pray and to Love: Conversations on Prayer with the Early Church*. Minneapolis: Fortress, 1991.
Bonhoeffer, Dietrich. *The Cost of Discipleship*. Translated by R. H. Fuller. New York: Macmillan, 1972.
———. *Life Together*. Translated by John W. Doberstein. San Francisco: HarperSanFrancisco, 1954.
Boyle, Gregory. *Tattoos on the Heart*. New York: Simon & Schuster, 2010.
Brinkley, Douglas. "Bob Dylan Has a Lot on His Mind." *New York Times*, June 12, 2020.
Brother Lawrence. *Practice of the Presence of God*. Translated by E. M. Blaiklock. Nashville: Nelson, 1981.
Brower, Kate Anderson. "The Simple Way Jimmy and Rosalyn Carter Live Their Lives and Values." *CNN*, November 27, 2019.
Bruce, F. F. *New International Greek Testament Commentary on Galatians*. Grand Rapids: Eerdmans,1982.
Buber, Martin. "The Writings of Martin Buber, I and Thou." *The New Yorker*, Spring 2019.
Callahan, Annice. *Spiritual Guides for Today*. New York: Crossroad, 1992.
Capon, Robert Farrar. *Kingdom, Grace, Judgment: Paradox, Outrage, and Vindication in the Parables of Jesus*. Grand Rapids: Eerdmans, 2002.
Carretto, Carlo. *Essential Writings*. Edited by Robert Ellsberg. Maryknoll: Orbis, 2007.
———. *The God Who Comes*. Translated by Rose Mary Hancock. Maryknoll: Orbis, 1974.
———. *I, Francis*. Translated by Robert R. Barr. Maryknoll: Orbis, 1982.
———. *I Sought and I Found*. Translated by Robert R. Barr. London: Darton, Longman & Todd, 1985.
Chapman, Tracy. "Tell It Like It Is." *New Beginning*. Track Number 8, Electra Records, 1995.
Chittister, Joan. *Essential Writings*. Selected by Mary Lou Kownacki and Mary Hembrow Snyder. Maryknoll: Orbis, 2014.
Davey, Alan, and Elizabeth Davey. *Abba's Whisper*. Eugene, OR: Wipf & Stock, 2017.

Bibliography

de Caussade, Jean-Pierre. *Abandonment to Divine Providence*. Translated by John Beevers. New York: Doubleday, 1975.
De Waal, Esther. *Finding God in All Things: The Rule of St. Benedict*. Collegeville: Liturgical, 2001.
Doherty Catherine. *Poustinia*. Cobermere: Madonna House, 2000.
Dylan, Bob. "The Times They Are a-Changin.'" *The Times They Are a-Changin'*. Track Number 1, Columbia Records, 1964.
Ellul, Jacques. *The Ethics of Freedom*. Translated and edited by Geoffrey W. Bromiley. Grand Rapids: Eerdmans, 1976.
Erikson, Eric H. *Identity and the Life Cycle*. New York: Norton, 1968.
Farrell, Edward. *Beams of Prayer: Spiritual Reflections with Edward J. Farrell*. Compiled and edited by Lynn Salata. New York: Alba, 1999.
———. *Little Banquets for Ordinary People: Epiphanies of the Every Day*. New York: Alba, 2000.
———. *Gathering the Fragments*. New York: Alba, 1999.
Fenelon, François de Salignac de La Mothe-. *Fenelon's Spiritual Letters*. Santa Barbara: Christian Books, 1982.
Foster, Richard J. *Celebration of Discipline*. San Francisco: HarperCollins, 1998.
Foster, Richard J., and James Bryan Smith, eds. *Devotional Classics*. San Francisco: HarperSanFrancisco, 1993.
France, R. *Matthew*. Leicester: InterVarsity, 1985.
Gawande, Atul. "The Blight." Review of Anne Case and Angus Deaton, *Deaths of Despair and the Future of Capitalism*. *New Yorker*, March 23, 2020, 59–63.
Green, Michael. *The Message of Matthew*. Downers Grove: InterVarsity, 2000.
Hammarskjöld, Dag. *Markings*. New York: Knopf, 1981.
Hebblethwaite, Margaret. *Finding God in All Things*. Glasgow: Collins, 1990.
Heschel, Abraham. *God in Search of Man: A Philosophy of Judaism*. New York: Noonday, 1976.
Lumière, Louis, dir. and prod. *Exiting the Factory*. Released March 22, 1895.
John of the Cross, Saint. *The Collected Works of St. John of the Cross*. Translated by Kieran Kavanaugh and Otilio Rodriguez. Washington, DC: ICS, 1991.
Juliana of Norwich. *Revelations of Divine Love*. Translated by M. L. del Mastro. Garden City, NY: Doubleday, 1977.
Kavanaugh, Kieran. *Collected Works of St. John*. Washington: ICS Publications, 1991.
Keating, Thomas. *Dios se manifiesta*. Buenos Aires: Lumen, 2005.
———. *Domingos en el Monasterio Mágico*. Buenos Aires: Lumen, 2008.
Kelly, Thomas. *A Testament of Devotion*. San Francisco: HarperSanFrancisco, 1982.
Kidner, Derek. *Psalms 73–150*. Leicester: InterVarsity, 1975.
Kierkegaard, Søren. *Purity of Heart Is to Will One Thing: Spiritual Preparation for the Office of Confession*. Translated by Douglas V. Steere. New York: Harper & Row, 1956.
King, Martin Luther, Jr. *The Words of Martin Luther King Jr*. Edited by Coretta Scott King. New York: Newmarket, 1966.
Lewis, C. S. *The Four Loves*. Glasgow: Collins, 1980.
———. *Mere Christianity*. San Francisco: HarperSanFrancisco, 2001.
Marion, Jim. *Putting on the Mind of Christ*. Charlottesville: Hampton Roads, 2000.
McLeod, S. A. "Erik Erikson's Stages of Psychological Development." *Simply Psychology*, May 3, 2018. https://www.simplypsychology.org/Erik-Erikson.html.

Bibliography

McNeill, Donald, et al. *Compassion: A Reflection on the Christian Life.* Garden City, NY: Doubleday, 1982.
Merton, Thomas. *Conjectures of a Guilty Bystander.* New York: Doubleday, 1966.
———. *New Seeds of Contemplation.* New York: New Directions, 1961.
Metzger, Paul Louis. *Consuming Jesus.* Grand Rapids, MI: Eerdmans, 2007.
Milton, John. "Paradise Lost." In *Complete Poems and Major Prose*, edited by Merritt Y. Hughes, 211–469. Indianapolis: Bobbs-Merrill, 1957.
Mounce, Robert H. *Matthew.* Grand Rapids: Baker, 1991.
Newman, Cardinal. "Lead, Kindly Light." *A Devotional Sampler.* Orleans, MA: Paraclete, 1995.
Nolland, John. *The Gospel of Matthew.* Grand Rapids: Eerdmans, 2005.
Scott, Ryan Alan. "Manna and Mammon." *One More Thing* (blog), October 28, 2014. http://onemorethingblog.blogspot.com/2014/10/manna-and-mammon.html.
Palmer, Parker J. *The Active Life: Wisdom for Work, Creativity, and Caring.* San Francisco: HarperSanFrancisco, 1990.
Postema, Don. *Space for God: Study and Practice of Spirituality and Prayer.* 2nd ed. Grand Rapids: CRC, 1997.
Rahner, Karl. *The Great Church Year: The Best of Karl Rahner's Homilies, Sermons, and Meditations.* New York: Crossroad, 1995.
Rahner, Karl, and Johann Baptist Metz. *The Courage to Pray.* London: Burns & Oates, 1980.
Roderick, Philip, and Henri Nouwen. *Beloved: Henri Nouwen in Conversation.* Toronto: Novalis, 2007.
Rogers, Fred. "You've Got to Do It." *Misterogers-Misterogers Knows That You Are Special.* Track Number 11, Small World Records, 1969.
Rohr, Richard. *Falling Upward: A Spirituality for the Two Halves of Life.* San Francisco: Jossey-Bass, 2011.
———. *The Naked Now.* New York: Crossroad, 2009.
Rolheiser, Richard. *Forgotten Among the Lilies: Learning to Love Beyond Our Fears.* New York: Gaililee/Doubleday, 2005.
———. *The Holy Longing.* New York: Image, 2014.
———. *Wrestling with God.* New York: Image, 2018.
Sims, Steve. *Blue Fishing: The Art of Making Things Happen.* New York: Simon & Schuster, 2017.
Snyder, Howard A. *The Community of the King.* Downers Grove: InterVarsity, 1977.
Tillich, Paul. *The Courage to Be.* Glasgow: Collins, 1952.
———. *The Dynamics of Faith.* New York: Harper & Row, 1957.
Trueblood, Elton. *The Company of the Committed.* New York: Harper & Row, 1961.
Underhill, Evelyn. *The Spiritual Life.* London: Hodder & Stoughton, 1996.
Van Breemen, Peter G. *Let All God's Glory Through.* New York: Paulist, 1995.
———. *The God Who Won't Let Go.* Notre Dame: Ave Maria, 2001.
Willard, Dallas. *The Divine Conspiracy.* New York: HarperCollins, 1998.
Wright, N. T. "At Home in the First Century." *Didaktikos* 3.3 (2019) 14–22.
Yaconelli, Mike. *Messy Christianity: Christianity for the Rest of Us.* London: Hodder & Stoughton, 2001.

www.ingramcontent.com/pod-product-compliance
Lightning Source LLC
Chambersburg PA
CBHW070332230426
43663CB00011B/2292